Henry Cecil has become a cult figure in the racing world. Before the age of forty he had been champion trainer four times. With a list of over a thousand winners, and £6 million in prize money, new records seem to have come easily to him: in 1979 by sending out 128 winners he broke the record for this century; in 1982 his 111 winners netted a record £872,619.

HENRY CECIL

# On the Level

*Foreword by Lester Piggott*
*Research and story by Phil Rostron*
*Additional material by Richard Onslow*

PANTHER
Granada Publishing

Panther Books
Granada Publishing Ltd
8 Grafton Street, London W1X 3LA

Published by Panther Books 1985

First published in Great Britain by
Harrap Limited 1983



ISBN 0-586-06344-7

Printed and bound in Great Britain by
Collins, Glasgow

Set in Times

Dedicated to
my Mother, Julie, Katie and Noel
– H.R.A.C.

# Contents

# Illustrations

# Foreword

by Lester Piggott

I have known Henry and Julie for most of their lives. During my four years as stable jockey at Warren Place, we had a lot of fun together and a tremendous working relationship.

As a trainer Henry is very dedicated and conscientious which is amply proved by the results he achieves. He can give the impression of being casual and often appears as the court jester. His outward appearance, however, can be deceptive as underneath is an ambitious man determined to remain at the very top of his profession.

People wonder when I am going to retire but I am looking forward to many more years of success before I am turned out to grass.

Lester Piggott

# Introduction

by Phil Rostron

Hand on hip, head slightly tilted to one side, the swarthy, smiling maestro welcomes another charge into the winner's enclosure. To the ever-swelling army of Henry Cecil fans it has thankfully become an increasingly familiar sight. More than a thousand winners, and £6 million in prize money, have passed through Cecil's hands since he started training in 1969. He learned the trade in a four-year stint as assistant to his stepfather, Captain Sir Cecil Boyd-Rochfort, and was champion trainer in 1976, 1978, 1979 and 1982, setting a record for this century when sending out 128 winners in 1979 and lowering another record in 1982 when his 111 winners netted prize money of £872,619. He is a cult figure to the racing public, yet has remained a mystery. When I suggested this autobiography he set only one condition. That it should be humorous. He is blessed with a sense of humour that many would deem off-beat. But he is the equal of all the masters of the one-liner, finding more entertainment in a single caustic or complimentary observation than in a whole series of television comedies.

Any trainer will tell you that were it not for having a sense of humour they would never survive the rigours and torments of their profession. The Cecil classic was delivered during the post-race hubbub of Critique's September Stakes at Kempton in 1982. In winning the race Critique became a possible starter, along with stablemate Ardross, in Europe's richest race, the Prix de l'Arc de Triomphe. Piggott would ride Ardross, observed the gathered newsmen, but who would be on board Critique? 'Which of you can do nine stone?' laughed Cecil. Mercifully, Joe Mercer was available to ride! I had a similarly torrid time when trying to arrange an interview for the *Daily Star*'s 1982 Derby supplement. 'Ring me at 10 A.M. on Sunday . . . oh no, you'll be in church,' he said. 'Make it seven in the evening . . . hell, you'll be in the pub then.'

A descendant of the Cecil family which ruled England in Elizabethan times, Henry, while maintaining an aristocratic air, has not lost one human touch. He has at Warren Place one of the finest private rose gardens in England, and once, when hundreds of people had long since left a garden party in aid of charity, a car pulled into the driveway at dusk. Two couples, weary from their journey, emerged looking dejected when they saw no sign of activity. It had been a morning function, but the foursome's late arrival was a blessing in disguise. They were given a personally guided tour by Henry, and they left for home with a rose for each of their buttonholes, and in a substantially better frame of mind.

Two pattern race successes in his first season set the standard for a career which has blossomed so substantially that he now has no peers. Like the gradual winding up of a spinning top, his winner-producing factory has steadily gathered so much momentum that, throughout the rest of the twentieth century and beyond, turf records are likely to fall like ninepins.

One of his senior owners observed: 'Having just reached the age of forty, he has to be regarded as quite simply one of the best trainers of racehorses of all time.' When Lester Piggott joined forces with Cecil at the start of the 1981 season the most awe-inspiring partnership of modern times was forged. The world's greatest jockey riding the horses handled by Britain's most successful trainer was bound to bear rich fruit. And so it has proved. Fruitful partnerships have been the feature of Cecil's life. He was destined to be brought up in the magnificent environs of the senior royal trainer; he married Julie, daughter of another royal trainer, the legendary Sir Noel Murless; he has attracted a collection of owners straight out of Debrett. Some of his owners wanted to make their contributions to this book, and here is what they had to say:

'Henry, who has been training for me since his father-in-law, Sir Noel Murless, retired, is thoroughly dedicated to his job, is a great worker and has built up a very efficient staff with whom there is a great deal of mutual appreciation. They work together in perfect harmony. Out of the few horses I have with him he generally manages to win me a race or two each year, and in recent years he has won me a couple of classic races to celebrate. Besides being great fun to train with, he does not mind if one states what one thinks. I am sure his wife Julie, who rides out every day, must be the greatest help to him. I wish Henry the continuation of the success he has already achieved, and hope he may achieve the ambition of all in this game by winning the Derby.' – JIM JOEL

'Externally Henry conveys the impression of light-hearted casualness and a somewhat haphazard approach to the running of his yard. This is totally false. In his mind is a clear picture of every horse therein, its proven or potential ability, how long it is likely to take to come to hand and a programme of possible races. Additionally if, over a reasonable period, he feels it is unlikely to achieve average ability, he suggests its removal. His great enthusiasm and outgoing and friendly manner endear him to his staff, and this has made it possible for him to recruit the very best who, once in the yard, seldom leave. He listens to what they tell him and leaves them in no doubt that due notice will be taken of their views. His relationship with the head lads of the subdivisions of the establishment, his assistants and the supervising head lad are an example of how to give and receive respect and loyalty from those closely associated in a common endeavour. His ability to cope, I am sure, is due to a secure family life and a wife who shares his affection and interest in the horses, plus the benefit of his two other great loves – wildlife and his garden. The latter is where he can be found whenever he has a spare half-hour, and in all the seasons of the year it has only to be seen to realize how much care and thought goes into it. I suppose my treasured memory of him is knowing how much he dislikes imparting bad news, something which is a very frequent occurrence to all racehorse trainers. During a time when my horses were very much out of form I received the following letter in the post: "Before you read further, there is no scare. In fact, for a change, luck might have been on your side! This morning Twenty Two stumbled and got loose and ran into a wicker fence. She has a few cuts and bruises, but nothing is broken. We shall have to give her an easy week, but in seven days' time she should be back to steady exercise. It could have been worse, and she will live to fight another day. Otherwise all well." Her wounds took rather longer to heal, but Henry showed how, even during a difficult period, it was possible to look on the bright side of yet another setback.' – LOUIS FREEDMAN

'I have known both Henry and his wife Julie since they were children. Although he was pretty wild when he was young, he always had a great deal of charm, and I honestly believe that this quality has an effect on his horses. To put it another way he has, in gardening terms, green fingers, and it can hardly be a coincidence that his other great interest is his garden, and particularly his roses. When I first trained with Henry my first two runners were winners at Newmarket. He knows pretty early what sort of horse he has. One notable exception was Kris, who started racing at Leicester and Folkestone before going on to higher things. However, some horses do improve tremendously and change everybody's ideas. Henry is very dedicated and, in my opinion, is just as interested in his less good animals as his stars. People often remark that he does not watch his horses run – but Julie does. I think Henry believes he has done what he can when the jockey mounts, and therefore the rest is out of his hands. However, he does watch the video at home.' – LORD HOWARD DE WALDEN

'I am very fond of Julie and wanted her to win the Ladies' race at Ascot on the day of the King George. Therefore I asked Henry to enter my horse, Tahitian King, in the race. He told me that Tahitian King was booked for a race three weeks before. I objected to him that the race was worth £4,000, and that the horse would not be qualified for the Ascot race. He replied that this would be unfair to the horse, and that he preferred to have trouble with his family rather than to act against the career of one of his horses.' – DANIEL WILDENSTEIN

# 1
## *Saints and Sinners*

Ten minutes after I was born in a hospital near Aberdeen on 11 January 1943, my identical twin, David, followed me into this world. Thus within less than a quarter of an hour the responsibility weighing upon our widowed mother had doubled, for she already had two other small sons. A fortnight before our birth our father had been killed in action with the Parachute Regiment in North Africa at the age of twenty-eight and recommended for the award of a posthumous Victoria Cross, while earlier in the fighting our mother had lost two dearly loved brothers. The only mercy shown her in the war was the failure to explode of the bomb that dropped on the doorstep of the house in which she was struggling to bring up her infant family.

My mother is Elizabeth Rohays Mary, daughter of Major-General Sir James Burnett, thirteenth Baronet of Leys. No man, I suspect, can be trusted to be objective about his mother, but those who knew mine when she was a young woman will insist that I do her a great deal less than justice if I fail to describe her as a beauty. Her hair was a delicate shade of red, lit up by something of the texture of gold, and her features regular beneath flawless white skin, with the laughter in her vivid blue eyes holding the key to her personality.

Her first husband was the Hon. Henry Kerr Auchmuty Cecil, younger brother of Lord Amherst of Hackney. While a regular soldier in the Welsh Guards before the outbreak of war he had had horses with the Hon. George Lambton, and in partnership with his trainer had owned a very good filly called Celestial Way, winner of the Cheveley Park Stakes in 1936.

The Cecil family originated in Wales, and the first to come into prominence was a soldier from the border country, who fought for Henry, Earl of Richmond on Bosworth Field in 1485 before becoming Member of Parliament for Stamford. It was his grandson William, later created Lord Burghley, who served Queen Elizabeth I as Secretary of State. Robert, his son by his second wife, became Earl of Salisbury, and was always known as the 'Crookback Earl'. He followed his father in the office of Secretary of State, while Thomas, Burghley's son by his first marriage, was created Earl of Exeter and became influential as president of the Council for the North. We are descended from the Earls of Exeter.

Strongbow (always known as Bow), my eldest brother, was six when our mother was left a widow, and Jamie, her second son, just three. Showing the courage characteristic of her father and brothers, Mother set about the job of bringing up four young sons. Engaging a nanny to introduce an element of order into the life of the family, she left her father's home, the twelfth-century Crathes Castle near the banks of the Dee in Kincardineshire, and went to live at Gesyns Farm (which our father had bought shortly before his death) at Wickhambrook, near Newmarket.

As her husband had had horses in training in the town, Rohays Cecil was readily accepted into what remained of the Newmarket racing community. With almost all the younger men away on service in the Forces, and the inevitable shortages and restrictions of wartime, life presented a dreary contrast to the one she had shared with her husband in pre-war days but, with her usual resilience, Mother made the best of things. In brief respites from looking after four young sons she moved in a constricted social circle, dominated by people in late middle age, with the Freemason Lodge trainer Captain Boyd-Rochfort one of the few bachelors in evidence.

At fifty-six years of age Cecil Boyd-Rochfort was still a

remarkably handsome man, with absolutely perfect manners and a presence that owed as much to the strength of his personality as to his impressive height and the military bearing that he was to retain deep into old age. For very many years he had been regarded as the most eligible bachelor in Newmarket, and there had been few hostesses who had not prized his presence at their dinner parties. At the time when Lillie Langtry had been the only person in the area with a motor-car she had been accustomed to send her chauffeur to bring him to dine at Regal Lodge, Kentford. While fully appreciative of such hospitality and forming friendships with a number of women, unmarried and married, Captain Boyd-Rochfort had always been careful not to allow those relationships to develop into attachments. Remaining at the apex of his profession, it seemed, was at all times his primary consideration.

Cecil was the third son of Major Hamilton Boyd-Rochfort of the 15th Hussars, and together with his brothers and sisters he had been brought up by their mother after the death of their father at the age of forty-six in 1891. Their home was a fine Georgian house flanked by stables and a large conservatory set in Middleton Park near Mullingar in County Westmeath, where the family owned property of considerable acreage.

Having been brought up among racing people in Ireland, and made friends of some of the sons of racing-men at Eton, Cecil Boyd-Rochfort at nineteen became pupil-assistant to his fellow-Irishman Atty Persse at Grateley in Wiltshire in 1906. Subsequently he acted as assistant to Captain R. H. Dewhurst at Bedford Lodge, Newmarket. Then while still no more than twenty-five he was appointed racing manager to Sir Ernest Cassel, the millionaire financier, whose horses were trained at Moulton Paddocks, a private stable on top of Newmarket's Warren Hill.

During the First World War Cecil Boyd-Rochfort

served with distinction as a captain in the Scots Guards, was wounded and awarded the Croix de Guerre. Five years after the end of the war he commenced training at Freemason Lodge with £6,000 borrowed from his mother and his American patron, Marshall Field. Success was quick in materializing, as Field's Golden Corn became his first big-race winner when she beat Black Gown by six lengths in Newmarket's July Cup. Within half a dozen years the Captain had laid the foundations of his reputation by winning races like the Irish Oaks with Amethystine (1924), the City and Suburban with Greek Bachelor (1925) and both the Eclipse with Royal Minstrel and the Cambridgeshire with Double Life in 1929, so that by the outbreak of the Second World War ten years later Freemason Lodge was one of the most powerful stables in the country. Many of the richest people in England and the United States had their horses trained there, and the Captain had been leading trainer in 1937, and again in 1938.

Jealousy is a vice never long out of fashion at Newmarket, and the enormous success of Captain Boyd-Rochfort ensured that he was not immune from the jibes that it inspires. They used to say that he had come to the town with nothing to his name but a bicycle, for no better reason than that he was often to be seen riding one as he never learned to drive a car. Rumour had it that he did not really know anything about horses, that he was heavily reliant upon his lads and that assiduously cultivated social contacts were responsible for his regular intake of high-class yearlings.

For his part Captain Boyd-Rochfort made it plain that he wished to keep his distance from anybody lacking the most impeccable antecedents, and was never to be seen in either of the town's fashionable racing clubs. He thereby earned a reputation for being pompous and humourless among the more raffish element of Newmarket society.

The latter delighted in putting thunder-flashes through his letter-box, and impersonating his owners on the telephone. 'What shall we do after dinner: play cards or ring up Boyd-Rochfort?' was a question often asked in the houses of some of the less reputable members of the racing community.

To win a bet Tommy Weston, the jockey, once rang him up saying in an American accent 'Testing transatlantic lines, testing transatlantic lines, repeat after me "I cannot eat."'

'I cannot eat,' said the Captain.

'Testing transatlantic lines' went on Tommy. 'Repeat after me: "I cannot eat my currant bun."'

'I cannot eat my currant bun,' boomed back the 'echo'.

'Then you know what you can do with it, Captain!'

The story of that telephone call, like those of other practical jokes played upon the Captain, was quickly embroidered as it circulated among the pubs and clubs. Much of the other gossip about the Freemason Lodge trainer concerned his betting coups, real or imaginary. Although the patrons of the stables were men and women of the highest social standing and utmost rectitude, it was common knowledge that its winners were invariably well backed even when their recent form was far from encouraging.

To everybody except his close friends, Captain Boyd-Rochfort was an enigma. All questions about his horses were deflected by replies that were as uninformative as they were bland, and although he was continuously in the public eye few people felt they knew him at all well.

The arrival of Rohays Cecil in the bleak days of the war had a quite unexpected effect on the hitherto somewhat remote but punctiliously correct Captain Boyd-Rochfort. She had been fascinated by the extraordinary stories that were told about him, and he became captivated by her. Although Gesyns Farm is twelve miles from Freemason

Lodge, he covered the twenty-four miles there and back three or four times a week on his bicycle to court her. Finally he became my stepfather by marrying her at the age of fifty-seven on 24 July 1944.

To have had two baby boys just over a year old, and two older boys capable of making their presence felt to still greater effect, at Freemason Lodge must have made a big and not necessarily welcome change in the way of life of Captain Boyd-Rochfort (whom we called Uncle Cecil). As I grew up I became ever more in awe of him. Although unfailingly courteous to his friends and his owners, he could be formidable when small boys had exhausted the patience with which he was not liberally endowed. 'Be quiet! You'll frighten the horses!' was a frequent admonition. A stricter man could not be imagined, and my brothers and I were always relieved when it was time for a meal, as he took a great pleasure in his food, and was always calmer and more mellow at table. One of the treats that he most enjoyed giving us entailed his buying a huge basket of plums, placing it on the sideboard and telling us to take our pick.

Although the Captain had a most wholesome appreciation of food, he had what almost amounted to an abomination of alcohol. Owners, or anyone else, expecting to be plied with drinks at Freemason Lodge were badly disappointed. His usual greeting to visitors was 'You won't have a drink, will you?'

All in all, the atmosphere at Freemason Lodge was well calculated to overawe four young boys, and although mealtimes might provide some respite, it was to summer holidays with our grandparents at Crathes that we looked forward with greatest pleasure. We were always very excited when Mother announced that she was taking us to Scotland for a few weeks, and I doubt if the Captain was displeased. By the time that holidays at Crathes became a regular feature of our lives there were five of us, as my half-brother Arthur was born on 28 July 1945.

Crathes Castle stands in about 600 acres of woodland, and the estate is made up of a number of crofts, amounting to some 30,000 acres. How we loved those holidays up there! We would take the night Aberdonian train from King's Cross, leaving London about eight o'clock. For most of the night we lay awake, as the train made its way through the different counties, and the increasingly broad accents of the porters and passengers on the platforms told us that we were drawing closer to Scotland. Having thrown our sixpences over the Forth Bridge en route, we eventually arrived at Aberdeen at about seven o'clock in the morning.

The factor, Mr Birnie, and the chauffeur, Sim, were always there to meet us, and the first thing we did was to sit down to a fantastic Aberdeen kipper at a nearby hotel. After that we set out on the fourteen-mile journey along the Deeside road to Crathes.

There was always plenty to do at Crathes. The keepers used to take us walking up grouse most mornings, and pigeon-shooting in the evenings. Then there was a good deal of shooting on the lake and along the burns, and on occasion we would make the higher ground and shoot blackcock and capercailzie. We even had roe-deer drives, although I never really liked shooting these beautiful creatures.

The keepers taught us how to fish, from the banks of the Dee. When we began to doze in the tranquillity of the warm summer sunshine they would attach a large dead fish to the end of the line, shouting 'Quick! It's a whopper!' Alert again, we used to reel in very carefully and proudly take our catch to the kitchen to be cooked. Fortunately, the cooks knew all about the keepers' ruse, and there was never a risk of an outbreak of food-poisoning in the castle.

Grandfather – who had served in the Gordon Highlanders – was always known to his friends as Maxim, because he spoke at that gun's staccato speed. He was a marvellous man, and as blunt as a rusty knife. On one occasion he opened the gardens of Crathes to the public and asked the neighbouring lairds (along with various other people) to tea. Included in the company was Mr Birnie, a shy and simple man, terribly good at his job and the most loyal person on earth. While the band played, and the other guests were laughing and joking, Mr Birnie sat immaculately clad in his tartan kilt and tweed jacket. Suddenly thinking it time to make a contribution to the proceedings, he timidly handed a plate to Grandfather, saying, 'Sir James, may I press you to a cucumber sandwich?'

'They are my bloody sandwiches,' said my forthright grandfather. 'If I want one, I'll take one.'

I produced no better effect on another of the guests. Offering a lady the choice between a piece of orange cake and a piece of lemon cake, I took advantage of her indecision by exclaiming, 'Too bad! You can't have either' and eating them both myself. This was regarded as the first evidence that I had inherited the traits of a family noted for its eccentricity. My nervous Aunt Ethel used to hide behind the curtains if there were more than two or three people in the room. After she had concealed herself one evening, Grandfather inquired as to her whereabouts. On discovering no one knew where his daughter had gone, Grandfather remarked, 'it does not matter; she is such a bore!' and behind the curtains Aunt Ethel remained for the three hours while everyone else was at dinner.

Possibly on account of having found so long a vigil behind the curtains uncongenial, Aunt Ethel duly appeared at dinner the following evening. When Scot, the butler, offered her the *pâté de foie gras* she appeared to think it was entirely for her consumption, and helped herself to the whole dish. Thoroughly disconcerted by the attempt to consume so rich a delicacy in such a quantity, she was soon spraying the table with truffles, while Scot as promptly made good the deficiency of a course by bringing up some clear soup for the rest of the dinner party.

A rather more distant relative, Mrs Harrison Broadley, must have dreaded our visits, as she had the unrewarding task of teaching us to dance. Since we had Scottish blood, we had to learn our reels by practising them in full highland dress. When after a short time we became bored by the interminable twirling we introduced our own version of the Highland Fling by turning Old Broadbeans around faster and faster, and only letting her go when we were quite sure she was off balance.

My grandmother was the economizer in the Crathes household. Her treat for us children was to produce a tin of coke – and five sherry glasses. Her own indulgence was to get out the tin in which she kept the stubs of long-extinguished Woodbines and take two or three puffs from one of them. When Grandfather died he left a vast selection of ties. Having decided we were too young to wear them, she locked them away against the time of our greater maturity. When at last she unlocked the cupboard to distribute them her sense of thrift was badly affronted by the flurry of moths that flew out from the decomposing neckwear.

There were three roads of approach to Crathes that amounted to six miles of driveway in all. Hundreds of the trees that lined those drives were blown down in the great gale of 1952, and whole woods gutted by the storms. Not having the resources to pay the cost of restoration, my grandfather reluctantly decided to make over the property to the National Trust for Scotland.

The original castle had been in the middle of a loch on the estate, and you can still see the mound on which it stood, as well as the stone inset with a ring, by which the boats were moored. It was not until about 1200 that the present castle was built for the Burnett of Leys of that day, high up on a hill overlooking the river Dee.

The coat of arms of the Burnett of Leys bears a hunting-horn and three leaves. The leaves are indicative of members of the family having held the office of Royal Forester, while the hunting-horn was given them by King Robert the Bruce in 1323 as a token of the promise that he would not attack the land of the Leys in the course of his conquest of that part of Scotland. The flag bearing those arms is to be seen at my home, Warren Place, as well as Crathes Castle, though we only fly it during the week following a success in a Group One race.

Crathes Castle is surrounded by the most beautiful pleasure grounds, divided into eight separate gardens by yew hedges dating from 1702, and long lime walks. My grandfather and grandmother were both keen gardeners, and together with a staff of about twelve maintained what are probably the most famous gardens in the whole of Scotland.

I have dreaded funerals ever since the deaths of those grandparents, to whom I was devoted. My grandfather's funeral was attended by a congregation of about four hundred, mostly employees and neighbouring gentry, in the grounds of the castle. My grandmother could find only two hymn books, which she unwisely deployed by giving them to my brother David and me. When the Vicar announced the number of the first hymn there was not a sound from the organ, while we, having no idea of the tune, could only mime ineffectually. Everyone looked very embarrassed, and eventually the vicar accepted the situation by conducting the service without musical accompaniment.

If my grandfather's funeral bordered on a farce, that of my grandmother can only be described as a shambles. The coffin was being taken to the burial-ground on an old gun-carriage towed by the elderly head keeper and some of his assistants, who were only a few years his junior. All was duly sombre until they lost their hold on a downward slope. Gathering momentum, the gun-carriage shed the coffin, and was only prevented from causing pandemonium by its onrush being checked by an oak-tree.

Worse was to come. Uncle Cecil had flown up from Newmarket, and volunteered to be one of the four men to lower the coffin into the grave by a rope. It was evident that something was wrong when he bent lower and lower over the grave as though mesmerized by the descending coffin. When we looked closer we saw that he was unable to extricate his wrist from the rope (still tightly twisted around it) and was in imminent danger of being pulled into the grave. Fortunately, we were able to call a temporary suspension of proceedings while Uncle Cecil was disentangled.

Back at Freemason Lodge Uncle Cecil engaged a governess for us, Mrs East. It was the job of Easty to teach us the three Rs, as well as to indoctrinate us in other subjects, of which I also acquired singularly little knowledge. Assembled in the makeshift classroom alongside David and me were Hugh and Geoffrey Van Cutsem, sons of the future Stanley House trainer Bernard Van Cutsem, and Hugo Morris, whose father owned a stud at Newmarket. At the end of term Easty distributed what she called Merit Presents. While Hugo would receive a geometry set or a slide-rule, my budding intellect was recognized by the gift of a Muffin the Mule puppet. I could never admit that either of the Van Cutsem brothers was any more intelligent than I, but I cannot deny that they concentrated on their work very much harder. This, I think, was accounted for by the fact that their father was apt to operate a still more oppressive regime than the Captain. Well do I recall Geoffrey Van Cutsem, in floods of tears, telling us that he was sent to bed immediately after putting his shirt-sleeve in his soup by mistake.

As a result of having learned so little from Easty, David and I went to the Sunningdale Preparatory School at the age of seven as ill prepared for the formative period of academic life as it was possible to be. That establishment was chosen for us because the headmaster, Mr Fox, was a racing-man with a filly in training, and as it was close to Ascot, Uncle Cecil would be able to visit us frequently. David and I went straight into the bottom form and stayed there.

I had two claims to fame at Sunningdale. The first was that I was awarded my school colours for football, and as goal-keeper let in fourteen goals in a match against Ludgrove, thereby bringing about our fourteenth defeat in fourteen matches. The team travelled to the away matches in two old taxis. By tradition we would sound the horns all the way up the drive as we returned during the evening meal if we had won, while the other boys banged their spoons on their plates in celebration. I can only hope that the staff were duly grateful to be spared that racket while I was in the team.

My second claim to distinction was giving a boy in my class called Ian Ogilvy a bloody nose after we had been involved in a tug-of-war over my pen in the locker room. Ian Ogilvy is now a notably fine actor. When I observed his prowess in the role of The Saint I often wondered how I ever came to get the better of him.

Rex Harrison's son Cary was also at school with me at Sunningdale, and so was Prince Michael of Kent. I am afraid I did not like Cary Harrison at all, as he never seemed to speak to anybody. Since I was an insensitive small boy, it never occurred to me that he might be shy. I am sure we would get on well enough if we were to meet again after all these years.

We were all very jealous of the treatment accorded Prince Michael after he had broken his leg on a ski-ing holiday. As part of his therapy he was allowed to ride a bicycle around the school grounds, which was normally strictly forbidden. He made the most of the situation by tinkling his bell every time he came anywhere near us.

If Tom Brown's schooldays were anything at all like mine I can sympathize with his much-publicized misfortunes. I hated the compulsory nude swims as well as the cold baths in the summer, and resented the treatment to which our hair was subjected. Beside having to wash it in an indescribable liquid of very high density that the masters called shampoo, it had to be cut by the school barber, a tonsorial butcher who got through twelve victims in ten minutes using hand-clippers.

I did like the music master Dan Latham, who had nicotine all over his fingers and wore thick-rimmed glasses. On my deciding to learn to play a musical instrument he recommended the guitar. My incessant pleas did nothing to move my mother, but when I began crying my eyes out she finally decided to accede to my request by buying me a beautiful pearl-studded Spanish guitar, which must have been very expensive. After fifteen minutes of practice I became incredibly bored with the repetitive strumming of the strings, and was later relieved to be told that a maid had stood on it while making my bed.

Latham played the harmonica particularly well, and I decided that that instrument was more to my liking than the guitar. The course of tuition on which I embarked lasted barely longer than my practice on the guitar, for three very good reasons. Firstly, I found my mouth burned; secondly, I resented Latham's intolerance of the ineptitude of my early efforts; and thirdly, I was inhibited by his dribbling during the course of a rendition.

In my final attempt to master a musical instrument I turned my attention to the drum kit in the smoking-room at Crathes. My early attempts to teach myself the art of percussion did not help maintain harmonious relations with Great-Aunt Nanie. Inevitably she became the prime suspect when a massive hole was found in the skin of the bass drum.

Reverting to the subject of Sunningdale, whence my brief interest in music originated, I shall always remember eating the boiled chestnuts which were picked twice a year in the Chapel Wood as one of the few pleasures afforded by the place. The other taste from prep-school days on which I can look back nostalgically is of the strawberries and cream that relieved the unbelievable tedium of Speech Day.

Against these two items on the credit side of life at Sunningdale there was very much more on the debit. Discipline in the classrooms was strictly enforced, and one master delighted in the constant rapping of our knuckles with a ruler as a means of maintaining order. When the mathematics teacher Miss Patterson adopted this method of establishing authority I lost my temper one day and repaid her in kind.

David and I were very close throughout the miseries of prep school. If he were in trouble I would feel pain and sorrow for him and vice versa and, as a child, I cried a lot. At least one of the worst of the ordeals there we shared together, for we were almost unmercifully teased because we had to wear hair-grips to keep our pronounced fringes out of our eyes.

Some of the organized activities at Sunningdale were so ludicrous as to say little for the mental acumen of the staff. Each boy, for instance, had a plot of garden and was encouraged to produce the most colourful display of flowers, for which there was a prize. Every year that I was there the prize went to the same boy, though everybody (except the judges) knew the recipe for success. The night before the competition his father drove up in his Rolls-Royce, with a boot stuffed full with Sweet Williams and other small and gaudy flowers, with the result that an arid patch had become a blaze of colour by the morning. One would have thought that some of the teachers would have remembered not having noticed such brilliant hues in the whole of the preceding week, but every year their sudden appearance failed to arouse their suspicions.

To our way of thinking the School Concert was little less of a farce than the gardening competition. David and I plumbed the depths of the former activity by appearing as the plumber and his mate, and promptly forgetting which of us was supposed to be which.

Our days at Sunningdale ended in ignominy when we became the first pupils of the school to fail the Common Entrance examination into Eton. Uncle Cecil, as an Old Etonian himself, was not impressed, and sent us to crammers near Chichester where we were supposed to receive remedial teaching from a retired couple (always known to their pupils as 'His' and 'Hers'). Whereas 'His' was tall and thin, his wife was short and very fat. The question as to whether we were able to apply ourselves to studying never really arose. There were ten of us there, and we seemed to spend all our time performing domestic chores like shelling peas and polishing furniture, or alternatively we were set to work in the garden. Going out on bicycle rides for a picnic was supposed to be a great treat, but it was not much fun having to pedal hard with a heavy haversack of food on your back, trying to keep up with 'His' and 'Hers', neither of whom were similarly laden.

The object of attending the crammers was to learn enough to pass Common Entrance to the public school at Canford in Dorset, rather than to solve the servant problem for 'His' and 'Hers'. That David and I eventually went to Canford was in no small part due to there being so many people willing to go to great lengths to ensure our success. Most important of these well-wishers was Uncle Cecil's brother, Colonel Harold Boyd-Rochfort, one of the governors of Canford, and incidentally breeder of the 1946 Derby winner, Airborne.

Grateful though we were for all that Colonel Boyd-Rochfort and everybody else did on our behalf, I think we really owed our places at Canford to some rhubarb. David and I took the entrance examination sitting on either side of a narrow table with 'His' acting as invigilator. In the course of one of the harder papers 'Hers' came in to the room to tell her husband that there was a lot of rhubarb to be picked, and forgetful of his obligation to the examiners, he left to help her with the harvesting of it, thereby providing us with ample time to compare progress with each other.

In due course we were informed that we had both passed, but a decision as to whether Canford would accept us would be delayed. Much to our relief, we were admitted to Canford on the strength of the examination results, though suspicions about the similarity of our mistakes in one paper remained in certain minds.

Seven of the other boys who had been crammed for Common Entrance along with us also passed, but the discomfiture of the one who failed was increased by our being instructed not to speak to him. By what seemed to be the tradition of the crammers establishment, the nine of us who passed had to take 'Hers' out to dinner, and she duly ordered the meal at the local pub. Unfortunately, the menu she chose consisted of a heavy stew, an appalling suet pudding and three other courses entirely to her liking and very little to ours. Thus for an hour and a half the nine of us sat and watched her enjoy this indigestible fare to the full while we picked dejectedly at what was placed before us.

We were twelve years old when we went to Canford in 1955 to begin a period of five years that was neither memorable nor particularly enjoyable. Although temptation not to concentrate, and to pass the time in idleness as at Sunningdale, not infrequently occurred, I succeeded in working harder than I had ever done before. The result of this unaccustomed application was that I exceeded everybody's expectations, and most of all my own, by gaining nine O-levels. I did not take A-levels, and the nearest I ever got to university was the fourteen miles that lie between Newmarket and Cambridge.

The two aspects of life at Canford which I disliked most heartily were the Army Cadet Corps and fagging. Membership of the corps was compulsory. I hated the irritation caused by the coarse cloth of my battledress tickling my neck, and I resented the Major's preoccupation with shining boots to the exclusion of teaching us anything that could conceivably be useful in time of war. With great relief I came to appreciate a commodity called Instant Shine that enabled me to see the reflection of my face in my boots without an inordinate amount of polishing, and (still more gratifying) to deceive that meticulous Major. This satisfactory state of affairs came to an end the day my foot struck a large stone while on manoeuvres, and the shine of the toe-cap shattered like a dropped glass.

That deception effected by Instant Shine earned me my first black mark. Three black marks, which accumulated by a totting-up system like endorsements on a driving licence, earned a beating from the headmaster. The black mark awarded for the spurious shine on my corps boots was quickly followed by two more for other misdemeanours, and thereafter I became a regular visitor to the headmaster's study. Some of the grounds for the giving of black marks seemed to be so trivial as to be unfair. I once received a black mark because one of my socks did not have a name-tape on it. Protests that our nanny was looking after five boys while suffering from arthritis were of no avail.

To fulfil the duties of a fag one had to get up a lot earlier than the other boys to make tea for the prefects, brush their jackets and trousers and then clean and tidy their studies. Going about these chores was hardly a pleasure, and it was made doubly distasteful by the way in which the prefects revelled in their authority. I never forgot the resentment aroused in me, and when it came to my turn to be a fagmaster three years later I gave effect to my views on the system by asking little or nothing of my fag.

During my later days at Canford I found myself increasingly curious about what was going on at Freemason Lodge. Although brought up beside a stableyard, I did not have a natural interest in either racing in particular or horses in general. We had been taught to ride, but were of no particular asset to the local pony club. I never hunted, and was to be thirty-eight before I jumped a fence on a horse.

However, in our middle teens David and I went racing a lot in our holidays, and as my interest developed I began to ride out with Uncle Cecil's string. I enjoyed the racing at home at Newmarket most, particularly the Craven meeting in April, the first of the year on our local course. The atmosphere at the Craven meeting was always full of anticipation, with everybody anxious to see whether the two-year-olds of the previous season had trained on well enough to be able to reveal normal improvement on their early form. At home at Freemason there was the excitement of the owners coming to stay. I shall never forget the way the aroma of their fine cigars filled the smoking-room, or how I adored the marvellous scent of the hyacinths placed around the rooms and on the landings by Tom, the gardener.

Tremendous rivalry between the Captain and Sir Noel Murless had built up since Sir Noel moved from Beckhampton to Newmarket in 1952. The Captain never concealed his delight in beating a Murless horse, and his pleasure was so infectious that we were able to share the pride in his success. A winner at the expense of the

Murless stable was always celebrated with a particularly elaborate tea at Freemason Lodge after racing, the principal feature of which was the big plate of prawns in the middle of the table. My brothers and I acquired so great a taste for prawns that we used to leave the course before the last race in order to indulge ourselves in them before anybody else, and not infrequently there was no more than the lettuce that had decorated them left for the owners and the other guests.

Eventually a lady acting in the Captain's interests informed us that prawns ought to be eaten with their heads on, and unshelled. Primed with this piece of sophistication, we ate the prawns as prescribed the next time a Murless horse was beaten, and as we spat out the hard particles of extraneous matter we swore we never wanted to taste another prawn.

Eating was a ritual with the Captain, and as he insisted it was performed his way we always dressed for dinner. Among his favourite dishes were cod's roe, cauliflower cheese and Irish stew with the contents of a tin of mushroom soup thrown into it.

The people working in the house made life very difficult for the Captain. For the most part they were Spanish or Italian, and could hardly speak a word of English. At first he would give an instruction in normal speaking tones, but on finding it incomprehensible would carry on repeating it, while his voice became louder and louder until he was bellowing at them.

When the Captain did manage to make them understand what was required the effect was all too often spoiled by his failure to make clear how the desired result was to be achieved. Once, on returning from shooting with some of his owners, he took a number of partridges to the kitchen, and looked forward to his dinner with customary relish. I shall never forget the look of horror on his face when he lifted the lid off the entrée dish to reveal the charred remnants of the birds, which had been desecrated in the frying-pan.

Nanny suffered as much as anybody from that lack of familiarity with English cuisine. She had rooms in the top storey of the house when she retired, and her meals were sent up in a small wooden lift operated by a pulley rope. On one occasion she asked for minced meat for her dinner, and was given sweet mincemeat in gravy. She never complained, but there were times when she must have been very close to it.

The vagaries of the kitchen were also responsible for the failure of one of Mother's most original schemes for coping with post-war shortages. Lacking the ingredients for a chocolate sauce, she decided that some Mars Bars should be melted down to cover the ice-cream. It might have been delicious had the cook removed the wrappers.

Mother's favourite member of the staff was Arte Bano, a bald-headed, hairy-chested Italian bearing no little resemblance to Lord Goodman. He always wore a white shirt with a blackish collar and Italian shoes with no toecaps. His claim to fame was that he had played the accordion for Mussolini. Mother was quite alone in thinking that he performed brilliantly on that instrument. He was frequently summoned to the drawing-room to give recitals of *O Sole Mio* and the like, and we soon learned that even the most perfunctory of polite applause would prolong a period of excruciating boredom by eliciting an encore.

The Captain never had much luck in his choice of domestic staff. One of his butlers arrived with immaculate references but was instantly dismissed on the Captain's picking up the telephone extension and hearing him order a huge consignment of wines and spirits on the Boyd-Rochfort account. It subsequently transpired that he had a record as long as your arm.

Two of the footmen proved hardly more satisfactory.

While the Captain was away in the United States they cleaned his silver by the application of an aluminium finish with wire brushes.

By contrast to the long succession of butlers and footmen, Anne Scriven could not have proved more competent in her capacity of stable secretary, and I am glad to say that she now works for me. She did not have an easy time at Freemason Lodge, and her problems were aggravated by her office being two hundred yards from the Captain's study. Theoretically, communication with her employer was maintained by a telephone operated by a rotating wooden handle, but as they were continually being cut off Scrivvy was frequently summoned by the Captain bawling for her from across the yard.

The sound of the Captain shouting and the sight of him in a temper were quite terrifying. Only once did I incur the full measure of his anger. That was when I bought some white mice and quartered them in the disused air-raid shelter in the yard. Inevitably, they bred so fast that their numbers were soon multiplied many times over, and the Captain was beside himself with rage on locating them, his displeasure being heightened by the owner of the local pet shop declining to buy them from him. When the shelter was converted into a dormitory for the apprentices it remained infested with mice for many years, but by that time I had taken a temporary leave of Freemason Lodge.

# 2
## *Wandering Abroad*

When David and I left Canford at the age of seventeen in 1960 we had no idea of the careers that we wanted to follow. We certainly did not have enough money to go into any sort of business, and it was on Uncle Cecil's recommendation that we joined the staff of Lord Derby's Woodland Stud at Newmarket, in order to discover whether we had any aptitude, or liking, for working with horses. The manager of the stud was Colonel Adrian Scrope. He was a wonderfully efficient administrator with a deep understanding of pedigrees, and he had produced no fewer than nine classic winners in the first nine years he was there.

Although the stud was no more than a hundred yards away from Freemason Lodge, David and I both bought scooters to take ourselves to work and back. In my case this proved a singularly ill-judged investment of meagre funds, as my machine had been written off as a wreck within a few weeks, thereby foreshadowing the fate awaiting many cars in the same ownership during the years ahead.

A few days after our arrival at the stud Anthony Cherry-Downes began working alongside us. Always known as 'Tote' – a reminder of a childhood inability to say Tony – he was about six months older than us, and was lodging with Scrivvy at that time. A large, boisterous young man, with wavy brown hair and clear blue eyes, he could take a joke as well as he could make one, and it was not long before all three of us were firm friends. Among the many things that we had in common was the determination to become a manager of a stud of international importance.

We were dreadfully envious of the fine big Dormobile that Tote drove. One of the principal functions of that conveyance was the transport of greyhounds. Tote was enormously keen on racing greyhounds. Before long his enthusiasm had infected not only us but Mother, who used to sit in the back of the Dormobile talking to Billy Bligh, the dog-masseur, on the way to the track at Bury St Edmunds, fifteen miles to the east of Newmarket.

We did not make a particularly auspicious start to our working lives on the stud. One frosty winter morning, the first that Tote was there, we were more disenchanted than usual with the chores of picking up litter from the floors of the boxes, and sweeping the yard. To relieve the tedium Tote suggested we had a competition to discover who could throw ice from the water butt highest over the wall. I went first and cleared it easily, but Tote's chunk of ice landed on the roof of one of the boxes, and slithered noisily into the path of Colonel Scrope, who was riding along the other side of the wall, immaculately attired in hacking jacket, jodhpurs and the most impressive pair of pigskin gloves I have ever seen. Startled by the impact of the ice on the pathway, the Colonel's horse performed an elegant pirouette, in the process of which it deposited its rider face-down on the ground. Climbing to his feet, he complained of injury done to his leg, very far from resignedly, and very loudly indeed.

'How long have you been working here?' he boomed.

'Forty minutes, sir,' replied Tote.

'How long do you want to work here?' asked the Colonel in a tone more suggestive of menace than of any real interest in Tote's immediate plans.

The second question was one which we were to ask ourselves increasingly often. Our duties were both monotonous and demanding, and the financial rewards of little account. The only payment that we received was twenty-five shillings a night for sitting-up duty. This involved being on hand at the stud from seven in the evening until five in the morning in order to be able to summon the necessary assistance whenever a mare should come into labour. From 5 A.M. we would be off duty, and then at 7 A.M. begin another stint. I remember being up all night with one poor foal suffering from meningitis and unable to move, and having to turn her over every half-hour in an attempt to ease her pain.

The Junction yard at the Woodland Stud was the domain of Cherry Pryke, a diminutive man in his seventies who had begun working there at the age of twelve. He could neither read nor write, and looked the living image of Mr Punch. What he did not know about thoroughbreds was not worth knowing, if you accepted his knowledge at his own valuation, and I must say there were often grounds for doing that.

I knew we were going to get along well together when I first made his acquaintance while we were cutting back ivy in the yard. Fiddling around with the contents of a tin of tobacco, he proffered it to me, saying, 'Here, have a bite of shit.' Such forthrightness was typical of Cherry.

He was always grumbling about the way the place was run. He had a profound contempt for vets, and his opinions of stud managers and trainers were not noticeably any better.

One vet had tried various ways to cure a constipated foal, but injections, tablets and various potions all proved quite ineffectual. In despair he turned to Cherry.

'Shove a bottle of olive oil down its neck,' suggested the old man, 'and then run a bloody mile.'

It worked.

Another time, though, his inability to read caused a foal agonies as he mistook a bottle of Dettol for an elixir. Cherry was terribly upset, as he really loved foals, and was always the first to make a fuss of a new arrival. There was one in which he took a particular interest. By the time Cherry had finished teaching it to shake hands it was more likely to be a candidate for Billy Smart's circus than it was to win the classic races that it was bred to do.

Cherry's achievements on the stud were as nothing compared with his record in the First World War. He won it singlehanded! But for the short-sightedness of a particularly obtuse commanding officer he would have been decorated with the Victoria Cross and every other medal the King could have bestowed.

His greatest act of heroism was performed in the trench that ran between the line and the field kitchen on the Somme. The sergeant called for a volunteer to fetch a three-gallon urn of soup. Cherry did not have to be asked twice, and the cooks strapped it to his back as though he were a pack-horse, so that he could crawl back to his comrades on all-fours. Half-way through the return journey he came under fire as a result of German determination to knock out the fearsome new weapon that was bobbing up and down as it moved along the parapet of the British trench. Round after round flew about the soup urn until one pierced it, and Cherry Pryke yelped like a scalded cat as a deluge of boiling red liquid flowed down the back of his trousers, thereby earning him the dubious distinction of being able to present a scalded backside to the medical officer.

Pryke was convinced that such acts of selflessness should have earned him promotion, but he spent the war looking down on his officers from the ranks. He had more than one lucky escape. His closest shave came the day he was to have faced a firing-squad, but when it was his turn to be shot the dinner gong sounded.

Another of the stud hands whom I came to know well was Roy Burrows. He had been Uncle Cecil's work rider, and had had the care of that great horse Alcide, winner of the 1958 St Leger. Through a misconception as to where his duty lay, this honest and conscientious man had had his jockey's licence withdrawn at one stage in his career, and earned Uncle Cecil a fine of £100. I was still only a boy of nine when he had the mount on Osborne, who was to make the pace for the previous year's St Leger winner Premonition, ridden by Harry Carr, at Hurst Park in June 1954. Assuming that Premonition, the 8–1 on favourite, would win as he liked, Uncle Cecil instructed Roy to be second if he could. As it happened, Premonition completely failed to do himself justice, and by the time they were in the straight a desperately worried Burrows was looking round, screaming, 'Harry, Harry, where are you?' In the end Harry Carr forced Premonition up to win by a short head from Osborne, who was easing up. The Jockey Club held an inquiry and withdrew Roy's licence to ride for three weeks, while fining Uncle Cecil £100 for 'not giving Burrows precise instructions'.

Two of the other men on the Woodland Stud whom I also got to know and like were Tommy Secker and Alec Notman. You could hear Tommy Secker coming a mile away because of his amazing chest-wheeze. Alec Notman, a Scot, I found to have a delightful sense of humour, and it was a joy to work with him. A very fine horseman, and an extraordinarily competent second man (second in command of the staff after the stud groom), he is now Stud Groom at an important Newmarket stud owned by an Arab. He is in my opinion the best Stud Groom in the country, and responsibility has in no way diminished his charm.

The long-suffering Stud Groom at Woodland was Mick Ryan, father of the successful Newmarket trainer of the same name. He typified all that was best in the old school of stablemen. A perfectionist in everything, he was always beautifully turned out, with highly polished boots that would have earned the approval of the most censorious of sergeant-majors.

Two members of the staff did little to endear themselves to Tote, David and myself. One character, a former soldier, seemed to lead a very privileged life: while we were given all the dirty jobs, he managed to make his little chore of cutting the grass last the full day, so that the grass was so short that the earth was almost bare when he was running the machine over the lawns for the umpteenth time. When he was not thus engaged he was often away at a shoot, loading for Colonel Scrope (who was an excellent shot), so we had to do his work for him. Another man, who rubbed up everybody the wrong way, managed to be as irritating as he was gullible. After clearing the paddocks it was his job to drive the tractor round the yard while we shovelled manure into the trailer. One day he had annoyed us so intensely that every shovelful somehow missed the trailer and landed in steaming masses all over him.

Joining Tote in the greyhound business provided a splendid diversion from stud routine. David and I bought a couple of dogs from the Newmarket trainer Hugh Sidebottom. He had had one or two decent horses just before the war, such as Buxton, who had won the Houghton Stakes at Newmarket in 1938 before running well in Blue Peter's Derby, and the sprinter Musical Maid, the winner of several races. A great Falstaffian figure of a man, he had kept Newmarket laughing for years. One of his most famous practical jokes entailed his impersonating the butler of the then Lord Fairhaven and ringing up almost every one of his fellow Newmarket trainers to ask them to bring their wives to dinner at Anglesey Abbey. More than one recipient of the call was duly flattered, and arrived at the Abbey only to be told by the real butler that there was some mistake, as his lordship was in France.

The dog-racing at Bury St Edmunds took place on a

flapping track, which is one on which rules of the National Greyhound Racing Association are not in force. As a matter of fact, there was only one rule at Bury, and that stipulated that once a dog had won it had to continue running under the name in which it was successful. Nothing else could conceivably be called cheating, and what went on would have had the White City purists aghast with horror. The old trick of giving a dog a bucket of water or a pork pie just before it ran in order to slow it down was quite commonplace.

Dardanus, one of the dogs we bought from Hughie Sidebottom, had won several races under the name of Holly Park Wonder before we acquired him. We could not understand why he did not reproduce that form until we discovered his little idiosyncrasy. That was that he could only do his best from one of the two inside traps. Whether we were allotted one of these depended how well we were getting on with the executive, who could easily stop a dog from winning by putting him into a trap next to one notorious for running across its opponents. Fortunately, we soon established friendly relations with Mr Sponge, the senior steward, who would put Dardanus into one of the two traps most conducive to performance. Mr Sponge also earned our gratitude by his happy knack of being able to conjure up sandwiches from nowhere when we were hungry.

Training the dogs was a matter of trial and error. I remember it used to be reckoned that if one threw a cat in among them it would bring them on by a twentieth of a second. It was not long before we learned that, and a few other tricks of a very intricate trade.

The members' enclosure at Bury was somewhat less smart than the Royal Enclosure at Ascot, so that dress could be as informal as vests, jeans and Wellingtons. Uncle Cecil, as a prominent and much respected member of society, would have been appalled at the extent to which we found ourselves in our element there. Nor would he have been too happy had he been aware that we fed our dogs on the prime biscuits he kept for the Freemason Lodge pugs.

Mother knew everything that was going on, and one evening insisted upon accompanying us to Bury, despite my protesting that she would be happier at the theatre. Having accepted the situation, we explained to her the sort of clothes that were *de rigueur* and asked her to keep a low profile. Shortly afterwards we were staggered when she jumped into the back of the Dormobile wearing a leopard-skin suit and dark glasses.

Billy Bligh and Mother spent almost the entire journey chatting about his prostate operation, and he probably told her of his literary achievements. Billy had served his apprenticeship with the old-time jockey Sam Loates, and his claim to fame was a sixty-page work of genius entitled *A Stable Boy Steps Out*. He was so proud of it that he sent a copy to the Queen, and a few weeks later came up to us shaking with excitement.

'Her Majesty loved the book so much that she has invited me to tea at the Palace,' he said breathlessly. When the big day came Billy was bitterly disappointed on his arrival at the Palace to find that he was only one of five thousand guests at one of the Queen's regular garden parties.

On arrival at Bury my misgivings about my mother's incognito proved only too well founded. Despite her elaborate precautions, she was immediately recognized by one of the bookmakers, who to the intense amusement of everybody in earshot shouted out, 'What price Boyd-Rochfort's selected?'

Although Dardanus did not get us into trouble with Uncle Cecil on account of the rapidity with which he demolished the pugs' biscuits, he did involve us in one distinctly unpleasant incident before we sold him to the

Sackville House trainer, Arthur Goodwill – always known as 'Fiddler' Goodwill by reason of the violin he brought with him when he came to Newmarket to be apprenticed to the late Harvey Leader. One day Tote and I were exercising our dogs on the Heath by standing two hundred yards apart and calling them from one to another of us when Clive Brittain – who trains in the Carlburg stable at the present time – appeared a short way off, walking the family dog. As soon as the greyhounds saw Clive's dog they were on to it as though it were a hare, and had almost killed the poor creature before we could pull them off. We were full of apologies, but Clive was unbelievably reasonable, sighing, 'Dogs will be dogs!'

Dardanus improved so much under the expert handling of 'Fiddler' Goodwill that David and I became convinced that there must be something seriously wrong with our method of training. Thoroughly determined to master the technique of the business, we approached Hughie Sidebottom with a view to the purchase of another dog. Hughie loves a deal. There never has been a dog or a horse that he will not sell if the price is right for him (which he usually makes it), and he soon showed us that we were as green as grass.

'I've got a real flyer,' he told us. 'Come down at seven this evening and we'll do a trial.'

It was already pitch-dark when we arrived at Hughie's and were told that he proposed to clock a black dog over two hundred yards of a path along a gorse hedge.

'What a mover, eh?' he enthused, though we had not even heard, let alone seen, a hint of action in the total darkness.

'Where is he?' we asked, absolutely bewildered, but wary of appearing unnecessarily ignorant.

'Oh, he's too fast for your eyes,' laughed Hughie. 'That must be a record.'

As we were far from certain that the dog had not simply

ambled home, we paid over £35 with the utmost reluctance. On the walk home to Freemason Lodge we consoled each other with the thought that if our worst suspicions were borne out we would not be the first people in the world to have been sold a pup.

Thus did we spend our leisure time in two seasons on the stud, during which we obtained a thorough grounding in the routine of the establishment without being anything more than glorified labourers. In between the seasons I gained more valuable experience helping to prepare yearlings for the sales at Marcus Wickham-Boynton's Burton Agnes Stud in Yorkshire.

David and I took our summer holiday in Ireland. I seemed to spend the time upsetting everybody, including the senior handicapper of the Turf Club, Major Turner. Not only did I take his daughter to the Galway Blazers Ball without his permission, but on nothing more than her authority I borrowed his car for the evening. Having parked it in a taxi-rank, we returned in the early hours of the morning to find all the tyres slashed.

The Scottish dance season in the autumn was an even greater disaster so far as we were concerned. Its principal events are the Aboyne Ball and the Doonside Ball, and in order to attend those functions a large party of us travelled north. We drank far too much gin and lime in those days, thinking it the ultimate achievement in the way of sophistication, and behaved so badly that we were banned from every event of the Scottish season, one of whose highlights is the Ayr Gold Cup meeting. The Captain was far from amused. In fact, he was extremely angry, and we did not enjoy the return on the night train from Aberdeen one little bit, knowing the reception we would have from him on arrival at Newmarket.

I may have learned nothing worthwhile from those escapades in Ireland and Scotland, but during my time at the Woodland Stud I had made up my mind that I wanted a career among thoroughbred horses, and to increase my experience I went to work on the stud of Mme Jean Couturie, the Haras du Mesnil et de la Chaussée, near Le Mans in France. She proved to be a wonderful lady, with a tremendous knowledge of horses and their breeding.

A feature of life at Le Mesnil was the partridge shoots given by Mme Couturie. Her guests and their wives were always smartly dressed, and in their determination to be correct would wear the heavy tweeds to be seen on the Scottish moors in winter, no matter how hot the day might be. They thoroughly enjoyed those shoots, but I did not derive an iota of pleasure from the proceedings, as it was my duty to retrieve their birds. That involved making my way through a thick thorn hedge, and as I emerged scratched, bleeding and using the rich language that can only be learned in a stable yard, I was treated to looks of supercilious disapproval by the women onlookers.

I left a memento of my six months at Le Mesnil in the shape of a horse with a jockey in the saddle that I etched on a concrete path before it had set. Mme Couturie, I am told, regarded the part of the path bearing that piece of primitive art as hallowed ground, and everybody was obliged to walk round it, rather than over it.

The language problems and the awful food accounted for my leaving France after only six months. I lost a great deal of weight because I could not eat the daily offering of the slimy, skinned head of a calf floating in an apology for gravy. It is strange that a distaste for the food should have been largely responsible for my departure from France, as nobody enjoys foreign cuisine more than I do, and the more exotic it is the better I like it. One of the few ways in which I can relax at the height of the racing season is to accompany Julie and a few friends to one of the foreign restaurants in or around Newmarket. We can always depend on getting a good meal at a place like the Moat House or the Onassis restaurant, where we celebrated the evening after Wollow won the 2,000 Guineas, or the Chinese 'Peking' restaurant in Cambridge.

On returning from France I spent a short time learning about the anatomy of the horse at the Equine Research Station in Newmarket. There I succeeded in earning the bad opinion of Mr Roberts, the eminent surgeon, through my tendency to give an animal too much or too little anaesthetic. Not infrequently his equine patient would start jumping up and down half way through an operation, making it difficult if not impossible for him to continue his work.

As David and I were still without jobs when I finished my stint at the Equine Research Station we decided that nothing would be lost by visiting the United States, and not impossibly, something might be learned. In going to the States we followed in the footsteps of one of our ancestors, the eleventh baronet, who emigrated to America after coming down from Oxford in about 1850. He set up as a sheep-farmer in Southern California, on countryside where there are now townships, oilfields, factories, a university, Los Angeles Municipal airport, and as it happens a racecourse. On our arrival, in less prosperous circumstances than our forebear, David went to work on the Claiborne Stud in Lexington, Kentucky, while I imposed myself on Greentree, a stud owned by Jock Whitney, who had been United States Ambassador to Britain for four years from 1957. He was an honorary member of the Jockey Club, and had had horses with Uncle Cecil for many years.

Having obtained driving licences the easy way in Ireland, we bought a flashy Chevrolet. Unfortunately, I found it terribly difficult to drive a car with gears on the steering column. Consequently David ended up driving the half-mile to his work while I hitch-hiked the twelve to mine.

Perry Alexander, the assistant manager at Greentree,

became a great friend of mine during my eight months there. He was about the only person to sympathize with me when I bought a pair of smart suede boots to look the part of a ranch-hand, only to find they were two sizes too small. I have rarely been more miserable than I was as I chewed a Danish pastry during lunch break on a bitterly cold afternoon while tears streamed down my cheeks on account of the agony from my throbbing feet. I simply did not dare take off the precious boots in case I could not get them on again, and had to spend the rest of the day in excruciating pain.

The other time that tears came to my eyes in America was when my mouth felt as though it had been set on fire. There was a type of unusually hot pepper growing on some trees on the stud which looked like garden peas and the younger members of the family had impishly put them among the peas at dinner.

There were all sorts of new experiences to be had in America. I particularly enjoyed taking the yearlings by road to Florida, though it was tiring, and David and I each bought a 98-dollar Greyhound bus ticket that entitled us to go anywhere in the country. By this means we went to the King Ranch in Texas, where we were the guests of Bob Kleberg, another of Uncle Cecil's patrons. He took us on cattle round-ups, and showed us how to brand a calf. There was a knack to that which I never mastered, and more than once I was left with blood oozing from my mouth after being kicked while trying to turn the animal over. The daughters of several of the cowhands lived on the ranch, and we found it far more amusing to chase after them than to go in pursuit of a stray calf.

After a brief stay with Bob Kleberg we went north to Canada, where we joined some lumberjacks working for the Manawaukee Veneer Company. They had just won a big contract to build a village in the heart of the forest, and for six months we worked on its construction alongside some French-Canadians. Virtually the last log had been nailed into place when a very sombre foreman came on to the site to announce that our work had been completely wasted. Nobody had remembered to apply for planning permission, and everything would have to be demolished.

It had been a rough, tough assignment, and I treated myself to the luxury of flying back to Aberdeen first class. That was bliss after living in squalor for so long. The nearest thing to a bath had been a quick dip in a stagnant lake surrounded by moose.

By the time that we returned from Canada we were twenty, and soon found out that nobody wanted stud managers of that age. In desperation we promised Uncle Cecil that we would study industriously if he would pay for us to do a one-year course at Cirencester Agricultural College. To this he agreed rather more readily than we had expected, but on our pointing out that it was a long way to Cirencester, and a car apiece would not come amiss, he showed no enthusiasm at all for providing the necessary finance. The Captain always had very old-fashioned views about cars. He was totally indifferent to the comfort and convenience of motorized transport, never learned to drive, and always held to the opinion that the best way of getting from one place to another was by bicycle as he had always done.

In the circumstances we had little hope of his acceding to our request, as it would almost amount to a desertion of his principles, but in the end he did. Eagerly we went up to London to pick up our cars. David had a splendid Renault Dauphine, and I had a Mini. Immediately we returned to Newmarket we took them to Exning, a village two miles north of the town, to dine with Geoffrey Van Cutsem while his father was away.

After a very good dinner we decided to drive to Worlington Golf Club to meet Frank Chapman. He is a bit older than us, and managed Newmarket's Dunchurch Lodge Stud (where Premonition was bred) in those days. On arrival at Worlington Frank greeted my arrival with a friendly wave, but his expression quickly turned to one of utter horror as I reversed into a wall, thereby demolishing it and doing serious damage to the car.

David did not even arrive. He had taken a narrow bridge far too fast, and plunged spectacularly into the middle of a field, not only disturbing the grazing sheep but writing off his gleaming Renault in the process. In the ensuing court case Fuller, the Van Cutsem butler, remembered only one glass of sherry being served at dinner.

After that Cirencester could only be a disaster. We spent much of our time going racing, and the rest of it drinking. Our favourite haunt was the King's Head, and we used to drink so much there that we were rarely in a fit state to attend lectures. A typical day would start with breakfast at The Mad Hatter, where I got on so well with the waitress that she gave me double helpings, and finish with about a dozen of us playing roulette at somebody's lodgings.

The business in hand was studying animal husbandry, which I actually enjoyed, and learning to use agricultural machinery, which bored me stiff. One of the practical demonstrations of which they were so fond was the furrowing and ridging of a field. To relieve the tedium we jammed the ploughing machinery with a rock while our friends distracted the lecturer with questions about tractor engines. The lecturer then drove the tractor up and down the field with the incapacitated piece of machinery he was towing producing not the slightest impression on the ground but gales of laughter from the onlookers.

When Mr Garner, the principal, arranged for the Queen to visit the college he went to endless lengths to make the occasion memorable. So did David and I and our friends. The night before the visit we painted all the daffodils, so that the first intimation the staff had of anything untoward came when they looked out of the windows to see the gardeners washing down the flowers.

Anthony Perry was to cause worse chaos later in the day when the college forester was holding the silver trowel with which the Queen was to plant a tree. Suddenly Perry grabbed the trowel, the forester Hart tried to recover it, but Perry was not letting go, and Hart fell flat on his back just before the Queen came into sight. Fortunately, though, Hart recovered his composure in time for the ceremony to be performed to the satisfaction of all concerned.

Not all the disasters of that day were attributable to us. Efficient as ever, Mr Garner numbered all the people to be presented to the Queen from one to thirty, starting with the gentry and other notabilities at the top of the list and ending with the foreign students at the bottom. There were two things he had forgotten. The first was that he had not informed the people that they were to be presented, and the second was that it was race day at Cheltenham. With almost everybody away there, the only people to meet the Queen were five overseas students.

Cirencester Agricultural College is run on very much stricter lines nowadays, and if our successors enjoy their time less than we did, I fear we are to blame. For us it provided a wonderful opportunity for one last fling before facing up to the serious responsibilities of life.

So many things happened at Cirencester during my year there that I just cannot recall them all. I do remember three quite amusing incidents that were funny at the time, although you may now think otherwise.

The first was a group photograph of the eighty-odd new students. It was taken with one of those old rotating cameras that go slowly along the line. As soon as it passed on the students quickly went to the far end of the group and were retaken. The final proof on the College board showed a large number of identical twins, and in the case of David and myself quads.

There was an accident one day on the Stroud road, so all traffic was diverted through the college grounds. By altering the arrow signs we had buses and articulated lorries going round and round the principal's house, thus ruining the lawn and drive.

On another occasion we bought an old Morris, which we completely dismantled, and then moved it piece by piece to the principal's house. When he and his wife returned from their week's vacation it was to find the car sitting on their bed.

At the end of our days at Cirencester David and I came to the parting of the ways. While he joined a bloodstock agency I was appointed assistant trainer to Uncle Cecil.

# 3
## *Royal Flush*

Whatever talent I may have today I owe to the tuition I received from Uncle Cecil. When I took up my post as his assistant in the November of 1964 he was still as powerful a character as he had been when he had become my stepfather in the very early days of my life. At seventy-seven he had long been regarded as one of the greatest trainers of the present century.

His horses had been so consistently successful in the very highest class that he had been asked to train for King George VI in 1943. The royal stud had been going through a rather lean spell, but the Captain was soon winning important races for the King. Kingstone was successful in the Yorkshire Cup in 1945, and Hypericum in the 1,000 Guineas the following season. Angelola won the Yorkshire Oaks in 1948, Avila the Coronation Stakes in 1949 and Above Board the Cesarewitch in 1950. Then after the accession of Her Majesty in 1952, Angelola's son Aureole carried the royal colours to win the King George VI and the Queen Elizabeth Stakes in 1954.

The run of success enjoyed by Freemason Lodge in the 1950s culminated in Parthia becoming the Captain's thirteenth and final classic winner by landing the Derby in 1959. To a large extent all that success was as much due to the Captain's judgment of men as to his judgment of horses for he had been able to assemble a superb team of professionals in the key jobs in the stable. Bruce Hobbs, who had won the Grand National on Battleship in 1938 before distinguishing himself in the war, was assistant trainer, Harry Carr the most conscientious of stable jockeys, and Tommy Lowrey – who won the Derby on Airborne in 1946 – was invaluable as a work rider.

In the course of four years the Captain tried to teach me all that he could about developing the ability of a racehorse and then exploiting it to the best possible advantage. As he approached the end of his brilliant career he became anxious to end it on a high note by achieving one last major triumph. But luck was turning against Freemason Lodge at last and the horses were not of the same high quality as those that had been sent to him ten years previously. All the same, he studied them with the same intensity as any others that had ever come into the yard, and that amazing eye for detail was as much in evidence as ever, but because he was so close to retirement he delegated more responsibility to me than might otherwise have been the case.

Although I was still only twenty-one the fear in which I had once stood of this formidable man was beginning to diminish and be replaced by respect and affection as he became more mellow. He nevertheless missed no opportunity of telling me that I was adopting an exceptionally demanding profession, which would entail my having heavy responsibilities to other people, and that in consequence I should have to behave with a good deal more decorum than hitherto.

My first opportunity to demonstrate my newly acquired sense of responsibility came when the Queen Mother was dining at Freemason Lodge. The lights in the dining-room fused, and as we were left in total darkness I suggested that we should continue the meal in the drawing-room. As is typical of her, the Queen Mother made the best of the situation by doing all she could to help, and when I took one end of the table preparatory to moving it into the other room she immediately took the other.

Once we were more or less organized in the drawing-room I offered her what seemed the most comfortable position at the table, and we began eating again. A few minutes later I looked across at Her Majesty to see her face beaded with perspiration. Only then did I realize that I had placed her far too close to the fire. Tact and decorum were going to be far harder to acquire than I had supposed.

In my endeavours to obtain a new image I no longer attended the sort of parties that I used to enjoy so much, and instead went to bed in good time in order to be on hand when stable routine began again early the following morning. Once I did break curfew, and on returning went upstairs so unsteadily that I woke the Captain by knocking over the bowl of lavender that he always kept outside his bedroom. Another discourse on the behaviour to be expected of me was delivered next day.

While assistant to the Captain I was able to observe at close hand the qualities that had kept him at the top of his profession for so long. Outstanding among them was his interminable patience with his horses, and his ability to reconcile himself to even the most bitter disappointments. In 1965 we were hopeful that a couple of the two-year-old colts would train on to have chances in the classics, for Smooth Sailing showed promise of being good enough for the Derby, and Donated was shaping as though he might be a Guineas horse. After we had watched Smooth Sailing work on Racecourse Side one Wednesday morning early in 1966 there was a quite sickening crack as the colt pulled up. I was in tears as we looked at his shattered hindleg, hardly able to believe it had happened, but the Captain would not allow himself to show any sign of emotion.

The following Saturday we worked Donated, and after he had gone a furlong exactly the same thing happened to him. It is comparatively rare for a horse to break his leg while galloping, so it seemed quite incredible that two horses in the same stable – and those two the best – should meet with the same fatal accident within the week. I felt heartbroken, and I am quite sure that the Captain did too, despite his outward composure. But he consoled me by putting his arm round my shoulders and saying quite simply, 'These things happen. That's racing.'

As we drove back to Freemason Lodge he told me to make a detour into the middle of Newmarket to collect some herrings. 'They are marvellous at this time of year,' he remarked. He enjoyed his herrings that morning, but thoughts of what had happened to Smooth Sailing, and now to Donated left me with no stomach for food for the rest of that day.

The Captain was almost legendary as a trainer of stayers, and it was with long-distance horses that he obtained his most important successes while I was his assistant. In 1965 he won the Goodwood Cup with the Queen's Apprentice and the Goodwood Stakes with Gold Aura, who also belonged to the Queen. The following year he won the Goodwood Cup with Gaulois, yet another of the royal horses.

The best middle-distance horse trained at Freemason Lodge while I was with the Captain was the Queen's Canisbay. That chestnut colt was successful in the most valuable event ever won by a member of the Royal Family up to that time, when he beat Roan Rocket in the Eclipse Stakes worth £29,451 in 1965. As Harry Carr had retired the previous year, Canisbay was ridden by the Captain's new stable jockey Stan Clayton.

In the old days the Captain had been able to run the stable with the military discipline by which he set such store, and he insisted that everything should be done with the utmost thoroughness. He was a stern but fair disciplinarian, and at one time his had been one of the best-run yards in Newmarket. He was able to demand a standard that is rarely if ever maintained nowadays. There was not a twist of straw out of place, or a wisp of hay where it should not have been, and every lad laid his tools out for inspection when his employer went round to look at each horse in turn at evening stables. Before the Captain came into the yard the head lad would have been constantly in and out of the boxes to ensure that no work was being skimped. Some of the boys would try to avoid strapping their horses properly by rubbing their body brushes down the whitewashed walls, then scraping them with a curry comb so that the lines of dust would create the impression of the brush having been assiduously used on a horse. That ploy might have deceived the head lad occasionally, but never the Captain. If there was one thing you could not do to the Captain it was to fool him.

By the time that he was eighty-one in 1968 things were very different from what they had been when he was at the height of his success before the war and during the years immediately after it. The shortage of good lads was becoming acute. Instead of 'doing' (looking after) two horses each, the lads were doing three, and instead of riding them out in two 'lots' (batches), one before and one after breakfast, they had to go out in three lots. In consequence horses were being exercised for an appreciably shorter time than hitherto. To a man accustomed to putting condition on to his horses by giving them long periods of walking and trotting exercise, rather than constant fast work, things were becoming intolerable. Moreover, the travelling to meetings all over the country was tiring him, and I was sent out to saddle the horses for their races, and to represent him more and more.

In the circumstances nobody can have been surprised when the Captain carried out his decision to retire at the end of 1968. Accompanied by Mother, he returned to Ireland, where they settled into Kilnahard Castle, a mock-Gothic pile built in the Victorian era in Ballyheelan, Co. Cavan, not far from his family home at Middleton, Co. Meath. All his life he had been an enthusiastic fisherman, and he was greatly looking forward to long hours beside the Kilnahard Lake, indulging in the pastime that had so often provided him with brief respites from the worries of training racehorses. But there were no fish in the lake any more. The discovery that the fish had vanished caused the Captain to regret more than a little his decision to spend his retirement in Kilnahard.

Long before the Captain left Freemason Lodge I had made the acquaintance of Julie Murless, whose father Noel (now Sir Noel) Murless ran the enormously successful Warren Place stable on the top of Newmarket's Warren Hill. At the time when I became assistant to the Captain in late 1964 Noel Murless had already been leading trainer five times, and he was to be at the head of the list on another four occasions. As well as the Derby winners Crepello, St Paddy and Royal Palace he trained Petite Etoile and a host of other good horses.

As we were of the same age, doing the same sort of work, and living in the same town, it was inevitable that Julie and I should meet frequently at parties and dinners, as well as on the racecourse.Tall and slim, with the dark brown eyes of her father and hair of the same colour, Julie has never had any affectation about her, while people in a position to be far more objective about her than I can be will tell you that she has the best sense of humour in Newmarket. The more that I was in her company the more I came to like her. Such sentiment was a long way from being reciprocated: I sensed that she thought me conceited and self-centred.

She rode out for her father every lot, every day, and in the hope of being able to have a word or two with her I used to take our horses to the part of the Heath where the Warren Place string was working whenever possible. This manoeuvre did nothing to endear me to Sir Noel, as my palomino hack seemed to have an upsetting effect on a number of his horses.

The Captain was not at all pleased when he realized

where my affections lay. He seemed to think there was an element of disloyalty in his stepson mixing with the opposition, especially as the recent Royal Ascot meeting, to which I had travelled in the company of Julie and her father, had been as much a triumph for them as it was a disaster for us. As opposed to their five winners, we could just muster one second.

Tote had just come back from a spell as manager of the Greek National Stud, and was whirling around on the swivel chair in the office at Freemason Lodge one morning when the Captain came in with a singularly forbidding expression on his face. In an attempt to relieve the tension Tote inquired jauntily, 'Good Ascot, Captain?'

'Don't you read the papers?' was the abrupt reply.

Although suspecting I was far from being the favourite in a very large field, I asked Julie to marry me. I told her that if she would not be my wife I would go to America for good, and almost as much to my surprise as my relief, she spared me another journey across the Atlantic in a westerly direction.

During the previous months I had used all the guile that I could to make myself agreeable to Julie. She loves crosswords, and even though I have always thought them a great waste of time I would often say to her rather fatuously 'Do you need any help with the crossword?' when visiting her at Warren Place, and then feign the utmost interest in 12 down and 3 across. What did me most good was a pure mistake. When in need of a shoulder to cry on at a party one evening she turned to me, in the belief that I was David, and I was able to convince her that her problems were of no real consequence. Eventually she discovered she was talking to me, not my twin, and seemed surprised to discover that I was not quite as insensitive and opinionated as she had supposed.

All things considered, the Murlesses had been extraordinarily tolerant of me while I was courting Julie. My tendency to write off cars had become more marked; I was still drinking far too much, and generally made a fool of myself when I risked the displeasure of the Captain by going to a party. On taking her home very late after one party we found all the doors at Warren Place locked. In attempting to shin up a drainpipe to an upstairs window I made such a racket that I must have woken Sir Noel, who suddenly appeared in his pyjamas to open the door to Julie. Just as he was telling her exactly what he thought of young women who stayed out until the early hours of the morning I lost my footing, fell and landed in uncomfortable proximity to a very angry man.

'Good evening,' I winced.

'Go home,' he ordered.

It was all very hard on Julie. She rarely drank anything except Coke before we were married.

Our wedding took place at St Mary's, Newmarket, on 18 October, 1966. That sunny autumn Tuesday had been chosen by Julie, as almost all our friends and those of our families were likely to be free on account of there being no flat racing in England on that day. Lester Piggott's daughter Maureen – then aged five – was dressed in turquoise, and carried out her duties as bridesmaid admirably, watched by her parents and many other racing personalities. Among the five hundred guests were the jockeys Harry Carr, Willie Snaith, Bill Rickaby and Sir Gordon Richards, who was to make a very good speech in the marquee which had been decorated in the blue and yellow of my mother-in-law's racing colours.

I had gone to great lengths to have the bride's arrival at church heralded by a fanfare of trumpets played by two RAF men, but to my ears they made an ear-piercing cacophony. They were doubtless excellent musicians, but they sounded perfectly ghastly to me, for the simple reason that I had a very thick head. So far as our wedding day was concerned it was not just a case of being the morning after the night before, it was the whole day after the night before, and it developed into a catalogue of disaster.

A hundred people had sat down to dinner in the marquee at Warren Place the previous evening. Although I had had a good deal more to drink than most of the other guests, I dutifully left at midnight in the company of my brother Jamie, and we drove to Colonel Scrope's house on the Woodland Stud, where I was to spend my last night as a bachelor. While climbing into bed I had a feeling that something untoward had occurred, but before I could recall it I was sound asleep. The following morning the grounds for my misgivings became horribly clear. Looking out of the bedroom window, I saw half an Alfa Romeo standing in the drive. There was only daylight where the bonnet had been. This cannot have surprised Colonel Scrope, as he must have heard me drive through the wooden gates at the entrance to Lord Derby's stud.

I rode out first lot on the morning of my wedding feeling desperately ill, with one of the roughest hangovers I have ever had, and absolutely dreading the prospect of having to make myself pleasant at the reception and, worse still, drink champagne. It was one of those mornings on which one never wants to see another drink again. I was not the only one bearing affliction from having drunk not wisely but too well the previous evening. My best man, David, was almost unrecognizable by reason of the deep green pallor of his face. Even Julie was hardly in any better shape. She and her two senior bridesmaids had stayed on at the party long after my departure, and were viewing the proceedings through eyes that were scarcely open.

Having slurred out goodbyes, we left the reception for our three-week honeymoon in the Bahamas in a Rolls-Royce that had been lent to us for the day as a wedding present, together with the services of Caulfield, the chauffeur. When we had got no farther than Royston, some twenty miles from Newmarket, Julie complained that she felt ill, and asked Caulfield to stop. As my bride opened the door prior to getting out into the fresh air, the same feeling of nausea overcame me, and I slumped forward in my seat.

'Don't you think it would be a nice gesture if you went to see if your wife is all right?' asked the solicitous Caulfield.

'It's the smell of the leather upholstery in here,' I lied, dragging myself from the rear of the car in timid pursuit of my wife.

After our honeymoon we returned to no home of our own, but we shall always be grateful to Lady Sassoon for ensuring that we had a roof over our heads. She had horses in training with Sir Noel, who had managed the extensive breeding interests of the late Sir Victor Sassoon, and her company owned the Beech House Stud on the outskirts of Newmarket. Beech House, which we were lucky enough to have as our home for the next ten years, is a mansion standing in a large colourful garden that was superbly maintained by two gardeners on the Stud's payroll. It was a marvellous gesture from Lady Sassoon, for like most newly-weds, we had very little money, and we were also greatly indebted to my mother-in-law for having set the interior of the house to rights while we were on our honeymoon.

I was on the basic stable wage, and Julie was riding out for her father. Furnishing the house was a slow process, although our mothers accelerated it with a lot of generous help, and we used a hard saved £2,000 to buy the furniture and carpets of the previous tenant when they came up for auction. Julie had always had an affection for the stair-carpet, and was particularly delighted by its acquisition.

When I began training after the end of the season of 1968 it was only natural that I should keep the string at

Freemason Lodge, rather than rent another stable. As I went about the place on my first morning as a licensed trainer every corner seemed to hold a memory of the triumphs of Uncle Cecil during the previous forty-five years, while every time I passed through the archway into the main yard I looked up at the racing plates of every winner he had ever trained, nailed to the walls on either side and rising in column after column to the ceiling. I could not but be overawed by the tradition to which I had been made heir, and thought that if I could but achieve half as much I should be well satisfied.

The Captain had bowed out after being made a Knight Commander of the Royal Victorian Order in the New Years Honours List of 1968, and gone into retirement treasuring the lovely cigarette-box that the Queen had given him on his eightieth birthday. He passed away on 18 March 1983, at the grand old age of ninety-five.

# 4
## *Cloud Nine*

Impatience for recognition is perhaps the principal motive for taking out a licence to train. After three or four years as an assistant one begins to feel increasingly frustrated, while looking forward to the greater rewards and satisfaction to be had from running a stable of one's own. Moreover, one is tempted to suspect that there is little more to be learned from acting in a subordinate capacity, while remaining confident that one is quite ready for the responsibility for training a string of horses.

My aspirations to immediate success never materialized at all. I came in for a nasty shock on finding that I had launched upon far rougher waters than I had ever imagined, and very nearly capsized.

Looking back on my early days at Freemason Lodge, I can always sympathize with young assistant trainers who are about to take the plunge. Some will realize there is a mountain to climb. They hope for the breaks . . . for the right horse to come along to ease their financial problems. Only realism combined with hard work and persistence can enable them to make a success of their stables in the long run.

There is, however, a certain breed of people who believe that training horses is easy. They are the ones whom failure hits the hardest. A man of this type will have been introduced into a training establishment by influential connections without his having gained any previous experience of working with thoroughbreds. In all likelihood he will be wealthy, and will have hitherto sailed through life without experiencing much in the way of hardship. He thinks how straightforward the venture is going to be. He knows too much for his own good. He criticizes successful members of the training fraternity with asides like 'So-and-so's horses do not look well' or 'That horse needs a longer trip' and 'This colt should be sprinting, not staying.'

He goes to race meetings to represent the trainer (who is probably on his way to Annabel's or the golf-course), and refers to his employer's horses as his own. He gaily tells the Press where he intends to run the horse next time, what a difficult horse he is, and how well he has done to get it to win that afternoon's contest. He believes he is the owner, trainer, horse and jockey all rolled into one, and loves to receive the trophy. When asked what the animal is by, or out of, he breaks into a fit of coughing, or pretends that he is otherwise occupied and did not hear the question. He has not the slightest idea, of course, and to change the subject bawls at the lad to keep the horse's head up and to lead him round the enclosure. At the time of his outburst he is facing the animal's rear end, and is about to be kicked and maimed on the threshold of an illustrious career. What a tragedy for him and would-be admirers!

I am not going to attempt to tell you how to train a racehorse. I have two reasons. The first is that everybody has different methods, and who is to say that mine are the right ones? Secondly, I have not retired yet, and if by chance I am doing some things right, then keeping them to myself may help me in what is a very competitive industry.

Although I was already familiar with a great deal of the work, life became very different after I had taken over the stable from the Captain. Not only was there much more work now that I had to make all the entries for the horses, write regularly to the owners and do so many other things that are no part of the duties of an assistant trainer, but for the first time in my life I felt the full weight of responsibility.

I was responsible to the owners for ensuring that their horses should achieve their potential to the fullest. It was in much the same way I was responsible to the lads, as they need to be in a yard that has plenty of winners if they are to have a worthwhile share of prize money and good presents from the owners, to say nothing of the satisfaction that comes with success. Equally important, I was wholly responsible for the physical and mental welfare of every horse entrusted to my charge. Lastly I was responsible for the happiness of Julie and any family we might have.

Some men make the transition from assistant to trainer confident that everything in the garden will be beautiful thenceforward. They foresee a life of endless champagne celebrations with grateful owners, and successful betting coups. They are soon brought down to earth with a very nasty shock. Having been brought up in a racing stable, as well as being an assistant trainer for four years, I thought I was well enough aware of the realities of my career. All the same, I was soon faced by disillusionment that would border upon despair. Although there was absolutely nothing of the playboy about me any longer, and I was willing to work hard, I was to find it far, far more difficult to meet the challenge facing me than ever I had supposed.

My first few months in charge of the Freemason Lodge stable constituted the cold, dark winter of 1968–9, which was hardly calculated to raise anybody's spirits. The horses had to have most of their exercise on the thick covering of straw that we put down in the paddock. The staff with whom I started was on the whole pretty rough, but I did acquire a marvellous head man in Paddy Rudkin, who had worked in the same capacity for Teddy Lambton, after spells with Joe Lawson and Scotty Pringle. Among the lads under Paddy when he first came to me were several who had drifted from yard to yard like itinerant tinkers, their only references being on the files of the local police station. We were continually being visited by policemen anxious to know whether I employed anyone fitting the description of an individual who had thrown a brick through the Co-op window, or committed a similar misdemeanour. The turnover of staff was all too regular, but out of every four or five new lads one really good one emerged and remained. In this way the nucleus of really competent stablemen gradually grew. It took me a good number of years to collect the staff that I wanted and needed, but nowadays I have a fine all-round unit of such strength that any weak link is made to feel out of place by the others rather than by me.

A good and happy staff is essential if one is to produce educated and game horses. One can delegate so much more, and be in possession of so much more vital information, when the views of the head lad and the work riders are to be relied upon. What one learns from the lads is also of great importance, for it is essential to know whether a horse is eating up, whether it feels right at exercise, whether its droppings are too loose, and many more details of its life. Each is full of significance to a trainer.

One of the practices that I started in those early days at Freemason Lodge, and which I continue today, is that of having breakfast with Paddy at 9.30, after first lot has come back, each day. He and his wife Joy have become good friends of ours over the years, despite Joy's habit of burning the toast and over-boiling the eggs. Having breakfast together provides the ideal opportunity to discuss the way the horses worked first lot, and plan programmes for them.

Horses are the raw material of our trade, and I regard their acquisition, their purchase as yearlings, as very high on the list of priorities. Unless you pick the right animals you are going to have no chance of winning the classics and other races of international importance. You are not going to win the Grand Prix driving a Ford Popular.

When I began training we had very few orders to buy

yearlings from owners, and to bring the string up to strength we had to rely upon buying young horses as speculations in the hope of being able to sell them among our friends. Our purchases were made for around £1,000, a modest price even in those days, at Newmarket, Doncaster or Ballsbridge sales. Put into the ring after the sort of animals we buy for five figures at the big American sales today, those horses with which I started would not raise a bid.

I like to think my judgment of yearlings has improved. Certainly I have a much better idea of what I am looking for, and those who help me with the buying are looking for the same thing, which is a very considerable help. It is obvious that you will make a much better job of training an animal that you like than you will of training one that makes little or no appeal to you. After all, if at a dinner party you are sitting between an attractive, amusing girl on your right, and an ugly, boring one on your left, it is only natural that you will give yourself the order 'Eyes Right', tilt your chair and pay more attention to the girl on that side.

Tote Cherry-Downes is now a bloodstock agent and does much of my buying, along with Alexandra Scrope, Colonel Scrope's daughter, and Julie. With some two thousand yearlings going through the ring at somewhere like Keeneland, where some of the most important American sales take place, it is imperative to have help in sorting out the wheat from the chaff. I have such a hectic schedule that time is never on my side, with the result that I can only manage one or two days at each of the big sales.

We do not believe in paying fortunes for yearlings, preferring to stick to a good working price and thereby ensuring that nobody's fingers are too drastically burned. We like to try to ascertain that if the horse does not turn out to be as good as we had hoped there will be some sort of salvage value to be had by selling it as a stallion to one of the minor racing countries, or as a jumper. Big money will never guarantee big-race winners, and we have achieved a lot of success over the years with animals in the cheaper bracket. By this I mean the ones costing between £20,000 and £60,000, which are quite insignificant sums compared to those often paid for a yearling nowadays.

We have to work hard to find a potential high-class horse in the range just quoted, and I follow one or two golden rules of my own. I insist that the dam must have a good pedigree, which means that she comes from a family in which the mares have been consistently producing a fair proportion of good-class winners over a period of years. My theory is that if nothing much good has come from the mare's family over the past fifty years or so the pattern is unlikely to change.

I like a medium-sized horse with a good outlook – a bold eye and an alert attitude – and it must walk well. The best way to judge its walk is to let it move away from you while you are standing behind it. I like to see the tail swinging like a pendulum while the horse gets its hock right underneath its body, so that it has the swagger of a beautiful girl. On the other hand, I have never liked animals with small ears. I have seen very few good horses with that feature.

Buying a yearling calls for imagination, as it is necessary to envisage what it will be like in a year's time, for many an ugly duckling has turned into a swan. It is a little like planning a garden. You go to the drawing-board with next year in mind.

Having formed an image in your mind's eye of what a horse might become, you have to give him time to grow into it. Patience, as I learned from the Captain, is the crowning virtue. To rush young horses can only lead to disaster. To use another horticultural simile, forced horses are like forced flowers. Just as the stems of forced flowers are weak, so are the legs of horses treated in a similar manner. Such horses develop joints and knees that cannot stand up to the rigours of a season's training and racing. I often wonder what percentage of horses fail to realize their full potential because of the impatience of owners and trainers. Many horses must break down mentally as well as physically, thereby earning the reputations of being dishonest and unreliable because they have been asked to do too much too soon.

I have to admit that in the past I have been guilty of this terrible sin on account of being too eager to obtain results. You have to remember that when a horse is travelling at 40 miles an hour at full stretch, more than 1,000 pounds is being supported by one delicate joint many times in the course of a race. To have the limbs to perform that function a horse must have all the time required for the development of the necessary strength.

Since I started training, about half the horses in the stable have been bought at the sales, and the other half have been home-bred on the studs of their owners. In the beginning we were grateful to take anything with a mane and a tail from off the studs. Now we are in the fortunate position of being able to take our pick from the studs for which we train.

A trainer needs to have a good working relationship with his owners, and sometimes this can only be achieved by the use of a good deal of diplomacy, or even the adoption of a firm line. The most frequent cause of disagreement between owner and trainer is over the meetings at which a horse should run. An owner may be anxious to run his horse at Ascot or York for the excitement and prestige of having his colours carried at a big meeting, when the trainer knows it would be more in its element at Pontefract or Yarmouth. Obviously it is in nobody's interests – least of all those of the owner – if a horse runs at Ascot with no chance at all when it could well be winning at Pontefract.

Almost without exception, I have always been on excellent terms with my owners. When Uncle Cecil decided to retire he asked all his patrons whether they would be prepared to leave their horses at Freemason Lodge after I had taken over the yard, and thankfully most agreed, although there were a few notable exceptions. The Queen left both Castle Yard, a useful handicapper, and Zaloba with me, but after a short while wisely sent them jumping.

The forty horses with which I began training at the outset of the season of 1969 were by and large a moderate lot. For the most part they either had suspect legs or were not very fast.

Like the rest of the Newmarket trainers, I brought my horses into fast work in late winter with a view to having them ready for their spring engagements, but since I was inexperienced, I was excessively cautious, and mollycoddled them. For fear of breaking them down by overtaxing their strength, I could not bring myself to give them any good, strong gallops, with the result that they were never properly fit.

By the beginning of May I had sent out some twenty-five runners, was still without a winner, and more than a little worried. To put matters right I sent five fancied runners up to Nottingham, and set off for the Midlands in a party of three carloads of friends with a certain amount of confidence. That evening I returned to Newmarket a lot less happy than I had set out. Of my five fancied runners four had been unplaced, while the one of whom I had been least hopeful had scraped into second place in a handicap under bottom weight.

Sir Noel Murless was beginning to feel very sorry for me, and no doubt anxious about the security of his daughter. He never liked to interfere, but after watching my string work one day he told me, 'Your horses are galloping like a lot of old gentlemen. You must make them work!' I knew he was most embarrassed at having to point this out, but I have never been more grateful for a piece of advice.

I gave up going racing, because I was tired of hearing people say, 'Don't back that. It's Cecil's. He couldn't train ivy up a wall.' Julie went out to represent me at the meetings. In the middle of May she ran over a black cat while returning from shopping, and a few days later, on Saturday 17 May, went up to Ripon with a three-year-old called Celestial Cloud, who had been bought from Lady Zia Wernher and now ran in Julic's name. In a field of twenty-five for the Newby Maiden Stakes for amateur riders, Celestial Cloud started second favourite at 5–1, and was ridden by Bill O'Gorman, the successful trainer, to win by a short head from Author's Correction for a first prize of £1,094. The judge gave that very narrow verdict in favour of Celestial Cloud without the aid of a photo-finish, and however many times I look at the Press print that sits on the mantelpiece I cannot change my opinion that it hardly suggests that we did win.

Our luck had changed, but it was not until some time afterwards that I learned that we had got off the mark. I had long since stopped listening to the results on the radio, as I find it disconcerting to get bad news in such an impersonal manner, so the first I knew of it was when one of the lads said, 'Well done, guv'nor, your first winner!' on my arrival at evening stables. The nonchalant smile I gave him hid the fact that I did not dare let myself believe that he was right. I jumped into my car and drove as fast as I could to the nearest betting shop to check the results board.

There were tears rolling down my cheeks as I stood at the end of the drive to Beech House, waiting for Julie. And when at last she appeared, smiling from ear to ear, I simply jumped with joy as she drove up to me, hooting all the way. The thrill of knowing I had trained my first winner is something I will never, never forget.

Besides Celestial Cloud (who won two more races that season) there are three other horses that I trained in 1969 that I remember with particular affection, because they are the ones who really made my name known in racing circles.

When Primera won the Ebor Handicap for Sir Noel's stable in 1959 he beat Jim Joel's Water Wings by a length and a half. Six years later Mr Joel mated Water Wings with Primera, and in due course sent the resultant product, a tiny chestnut filly with bandy legs called Karen, into training at Warren Place.

Karen was a tiresome, temperamental filly who made a thorough nuisance of herself. By the time that she was a three-year-old in 1969 Sir Noel decided that he was far too busy training good horses to be bothered with her, and sent her down to us at Freemason Lodge.

We soon found that when she was taken to the working grounds she usually dug her toes in and refused to canter. Eventually, though, a mixture of gentle persuasion on our part and maturity on hers had the effect of inducing her to take her work and her racing seriously. She won for the first time when Geoff Lewis rode her at Leicester in June, then she went on to complete the hat-trick when awarded a race on the disqualification of Splash Down at Nottingham before winning by a dozen lengths at Pontefract. She in her turn was disqualified and relegated to second place after swerving across Pseudonym at Lingfield in August. Subsequently her temperament deteriorated and she became as awkward and uncooperative as she had been on arrival in the yard. The last time that we ran her she walked backwards all the way to the start when carrying top weight at Chepstow. Once she was racing, however, she ran her race out as courageously as ever, and responded to the strong riding of Stan Smith by getting up close home to win by a short head.

The two good horses we had in the yard in 1969 were

Wolver Hollow and Approval. The five-year-old Wolver Hollow was a strapping bay owned by the centenarian American Mrs Hope Iselin, the widow of a banker, who had had horses at Freemason Lodge since 1950. When Lester Piggott rode Wolver Hollow to beat Bernard Van Cutsem's good mare Park Top in the Eclipse Stakes at Sandown Park in early July I obtained my first success in a group race, and I treated myself to the luxury of thinking that I might not be as great a failure as I thought myself after that disastrous Nottingham meeting in May.

Sadly, Mrs Isclin died at the great age of a hundred and two the following year. She had transferred her racing interests to England from the United States because racing in England was 'run by gentlemen, and I am treated like a lady there instead of a business corporation'.

Sir Humphrey de Trafford's Approval was a two-year-old chestnut colt by Alcide, the horse with whom the Captain had won the St Leger for Sir Humphrey in 1958. After being beaten by a head by Tamil at Ascot in late September first time out, Approval went up to Doncaster for the Observer Gold Cup, now the William Hill Futurity Stakes. With Duncan Keith riding him hard on the turn into the straight our chances did not look at all promising, but once in line for home he made up ground steadily, and producing a fine turn of speed inside the final furlong got up to beat Great Heron by a length. A second success in a group race in my first season was more than welcome. At the end of it I was eighth in the list of winning trainers, having won 27 races worth £60,461, as opposed to the 35 worth £105,355 won by Arthur Budgett, who was first.

The season therefore had ended much more happily than it had begun, and had its funny moments. For most of the time the jockeys' championship was closely contested by Lester Piggott and Geoff Lewis, and Lewis looked like establishing a useful advantage from four booked rides at Hamilton Park, two of them on our horses.

Two days before the meeting Lester phoned to say 'I'll ride your two at Hamilton. Geoff will be at Nottingham.'

Seeing from the Press that Lester was down to ride both my runners, Geoff rang up in a somewhat bemused state to ask what had happened.

'Lester said you would be at Nottingham,' I told him.

'But that's a bloody jumping meeting!' expostulated Geoff.

In or out of the saddle, Lester's tactics take a bit of beating! He had never ridden at Hamilton Park before, and with the thoroughness that has made him the great jockey he is he walked the course before racing, and duly won on both my horses, Pride of India and Rain in the Face, as well as on two of his other three mounts. In the end he retained his championship with 163 winners as opposed to the 146 ridden by Geoff Lewis.

Hamilton Park, which is about ten miles from Glasgow, was by no means the only minor course on which I had had runners. Our motto was 'Anywhere for a Winner'. I took our horses to places which would never have entered upon the reckoning of the Captain or Sir Noel, and our car clocked 60,000 miles between April and October.

One day I had to drive to Haydock Park in Lancashire. I have never been particularly good at reading maps, and have often wasted a lot of time by losing my way. On this occasion I was especially anxious to make no mistakes as I wanted to be back at Newmarket in time for the twenty-first birthday party of Lyn Alexánder, the artist. Somehow I fetched up at Leeds, and was so angry with myself that I abandoned the attempt to reach Haydock Park. By the time I arrived home I had become so frustrated by further navigational errors that I went straight to bed and missed the party.

Many people, ranging from family and close friends to complete strangers, were extraordinarily kind to us during that first year we trained. When one of Julie's tyres blew on the Severn Bridge on the way to see Karen run at Chepstow, motorists jumped out of their cars to change the wheel as quickly as possible, and would not take even a drink for their trouble.

The Captain sold Freemason Lodge at the end of the season of 1969, as of course we had known he would, and the new owners demolished the dwelling-house soon afterwards. I was glad to see the disappearance of that big, ugly Victorian monstrosity from beside the tree-lined Bury Road. The four-storey, ivy-covered building had always seemed out of place next to the lovely yard, with the lads' hostel and large paddock behind it. We had had our own Jersey cows and a grand vegetable garden there, though Tom Woollard, the gardener, used to throw a fit at the thought of anything being picked. Woollard was very faithful to the Captain, and delighted in telling him, in a most confidential manner, everything that happened. My brothers and I were very fond of cricket, and set up a net in the front garden. Woollard was driven to distraction because the bowler began his run from behind the herbaceous border, which of course got flattened.

The sale of Freemason Lodge left us with a problem, as we could not afford to buy a stable, but the Jockey Club came to the rescue by renting us the Marriott Stables, which were in the process of being built on Hamilton Road on the racecourse side of town. Jeremy Hindley very kindly said that we could have the temporary use of the Kremlin House Stable which he had just bought. Then when he began modernizing that establishment we divided our horses between the racecourse stables and a yard over at Exning. At the time we moved into the Marriott Stables the walls of the boxes were still not dry, and the horses had a wonderful time eating through them until the place looked like a giant Gorgonzola cheese.

Our string had grown to around sixty by the outset of our second season in 1970, and Greville Starkey was engaged as stable jockey. He rode the winners of thirty of the thirty-five races we won, three of them on Rain in the Face. Having won the Dante Stakes at York, Approval finished seventh to Nijinsky in the Derby, and was again seventh to that great horse in the Irish Derby.

We were now beginning to think that the stable was making a real impact, and the following year, 1971, was memorable for several reasons. Charles St George's Orosio was ridden by Geoff Lewis to win the Cesarewitch, and a two-year-old sprinter called Affection, owned by Mrs George Lambton, won five times and was runner-up in her other three races. In all we had fifty-three winners that year, and to our great delight an addition to the family. On the day that the Gold Cup was run at Royal Ascot Julie celebrated the success of her father's horse Philip of Spain on the same card by giving birth to a lovely daughter, Katrina Henrietta Amherst.

In 1972 we were rewarded for becoming rather more adventurous with successes in two important races overseas. In August Philip Winstone's Primerello, ridden by Greville Starkey, won the £6,500 Grand Handicap d'Ostende, and three months later we took Charles St George's grey colt Irvine over to Italy to win the Group One Premio Roma, worth more than £21,000.

I had greatly looked forward to the trip, as it provided an ideal opportunity to buy some Gucci shoes, of which I supposed there would be a far wider choice at very much lower prices than at home. I was to be proved totally wrong on both counts. The shoes that I bought were not only more expensive than they would have been in England but they did not fit very well either. After racing I hobbled back into the Excelsior Hotel, carrying the wretched shoes, and thinking back to the similar extremes of discomfort caused by suede cowboy boots in the United States.

The same season as we won our first race abroad I

trained a two-year-old with something very special about her so far as Julie and I were concerned. This was the bay filly whom Nancy, Lady Dunraven, had named Katie Cecil after our daughter. She won by six lengths in the hands of Frankie Durr on Newmarket's July course first time out, and the only other time that she ran as a two-year-old was a winner at Yarmouth. The following season she won the £6,000 Prix de la Calonne at Deauville together with Ascot's Marlborough House Stakes and a race at York.

It was also in 1973 that the original Katie Cecil acquired a brother in the person of Arthur Noel Amherst (always known as Noel after his grandfather). Thus both my children have the name Amherst in memory of my father's brother, who was Lord Amherst of Hackney.

The fifty races that we won in 1974 included the Jockey Club Stakes and Royal Ascot's Hardwicke Stakes with Sir Reginald Macdonald-Buchanan's Relay Race, and four handicaps within ten weeks – at Pontefract, Windsor, Doncaster and Newbury with Peter Richards's One Night Stand, a chestnut by the American horse Gala Performance.

During the remaining two seasons that the horses were in the Marriott Stables we were to obtain still more important successes, of which I shall write later. Then, at the end of the 1976 season, an important change in our circumstances was brought about by our being able to move into a home of our own, with the house and garden adjacent to a large complex of stabling, cottages and paddocks.

# 5
## *Trooping the Colours*

Early in 1976 Sir Noel told me that he would be retiring at the end of the coming season, and inquired whether I would like to buy Warren Place from him. He offered me one of the most famous training establishments in the country for a very reasonable price, and thanks to that generosity on his part, and an accommodating bank manager, we were able to complete the purchase.

As we rode the horses away from Marriott, through the water course at the back of the town, and across the Heath to their new stable one morning in December, it occurred to me that I would be endeavouring to maintain a great tradition for the second time in a still brief career. During the twenty-four years that my father-in-law trained at Warren Place he had sent the winners of no fewer than seventeen classics out to add to the two he had won while in the Beckhampton stables on the Wiltshire Downs.

Sheltered by a belt of trees, Warren Place is situated on the top of Warren Hill, about a mile outside Newmarket. The pseudo-Tudor house and some of the boxes were built by Sam Darling with the proceeds of the coup he brought off by completing the autumn double with Masked Marvel in the Cambridgeshire and Forsetti in the Cesarewitch in 1925. Sam Darling was coincidentally the brother of Fred Darling, from whom Sir Noel took over the Beckhampton stable in 1947. His wife Thora took a great interest in the building of the house, and had quite a lot to do with the design. Maples were the contractors, and as the house took shape the local people derived much amusement from dubbing it Harvey Nichols, because its size was about the same as that top London store.

Panelling was brought from a fine old house in Norfolk that was being demolished, and it is now in our drawing-room, while the smoked oak surround of the fireplace in the hall is another feature of the house. That panelling from Norfolk is not alone in lending genuine antiquity to Warren Place, as the carved oak barge boards covering the eaves came from the barges recovered from the bed of the Thames. The yard at Warren Place was a copy of an Italian one; it is part of the stabling built by Darling, and has a roof of red Italian slate above large tiled boxes. Just after the end of the last war Darling sold Warren Place to the Maharajah of Baroda, who made the house his principal residence in England and spent a huge sum of money modernizing and extending the facilities, so that it came to be known as 'The Racehorses' Ritz'. A cottage was built for Sam Armstrong, who had come south from Middleham to be the Maharajah's trainer, together with several smaller cottages for other members of the staff, while fresh ranges of stabling were constructed to the rear of the elegant front yard erected by Sam Darling. During a very short time at Warren Place Sam Armstrong was responsible for the Maharajah's horses making a big impact on English racing. Not only did he send out the first classic winner from the yard when Sayajirao beat Arbar in the St Leger of 1947, but he also won the 2,000 Guineas with My Babu in 1948.

Soon afterwards political and financial difficulties arising from the recent grant of independence to India obliged the Maharajah of Baroda to abandon the idea of building a racing empire to outshine that of the Aga Khan. Sam Armstrong moved to St Gatien, not far from the bottom of Warren Hill, to become a public trainer, and Warren Place, empty and deserted, was put on the market. By the time that Sir Noel bought it in 1952 the property had really run to seed, with the paddocks and cinder track overgrown by brambles, nettles and other weeds, and the tennis court, once one of the finest on grass in the whole country, in an even more deplorable state.

There being no prospect of restoring the tennis court, Sir Noel took advantage of its sheltered position behind the principal buildings and had the site cleared and a fillies' yard laid out upon it. The only person to regret the disappearance of all that dense undergrowth entwined about decaying wire mesh and posts was teenage Julie, as she and her friends had become accustomed to using it for games of Cowboys and Indians and tethering their ponies at 'the ranch house', as they called the derelict pavilion. Within two years of construction the new yard was stabling the 1,000 Guineas and Oaks winner Petite Etoile, as well as the fillies that were third and fourth to her in that Oaks of 1959. Since we have been at Warren Place two more classic winners have come out of the yard – namely, One in a Million and Fairy Footsteps.

As a result of the number of boxes added to the stabling of the Maharajah first by Sir Noel, then by ourselves, and the conversion of garages and other buildings, there is accommodation for 124 horses at Warren Place. Most of the horses too backward to be trained seriously, and those on the easy list through injury, are with Charlie King over at Exning, and others in these categories in the care of Bobby and Sally Jones. Charlie King is an absolutely superb nagsman, to use a rather old-fashioned word for a man who has the knack of making young horses by teaching them good manners, and curing them of any bad habits they may have acquired. He was apprenticed to George Lambton, rode as a jump jockey for a time, and became head lad to John Winter in the Highfield stable on the Bury Road before setting up on his own.

With eight cottages and a hostel together with a canteen for some of the single lads, there is quite a community at Warren Place nowadays. The yard van is used to run the staff to and from the town, but the drifting snow and the ice made driving an ordinary vehicle such a nightmare during the dreadful winter of 1981 that we had to resort to tractor and trailer.

In the town there are a variety of amusements and entertainments to be had at the New Astley Club for stablemen, and other social clubs, cafés, coffee bars and pubs. Nor is life altogether without its highlights at Warren Place outside stable hours, as a group of the lads have formed an entertainments committee and succeed in providing a lot of fun for everybody.

Work and the care of the horses have to be taken very seriously indeed, but I have never believed that any of us should be so solemn about it that there ceases to be any pleasure at all. As I ride alongside the string on my Arab hack I like to hear the lads laughing, and chaffing each other, for I firmly believe that a happy staff makes happy horses, and that horses will never show their best on a racecourse if they are not happy and relaxed.

Ever since I was a boy growing up at Freemason Lodge I have loved the humour of stablemen, which is very often extremely witty, generally unprintable and sometimes unconscious. A lovely example of the third variety was heard in the yard last year.

John Higgins, who has ridden a number of winners for me, took a crashing fall on the all-weather gallop. Later that morning someone came to the yard to ask after him.

'He's fine,' said a boy we call Rabbit. 'He only fell on his head.'

By long tradition lads have given apprentices stable names on their arrival. Very often those names stay with them for the rest of their lives, no matter how many times they move from one yard to another, and their Christian names are quite forgotten by all save their family. Most stable names like Cockney, Manch, Sheff – Harry Wragg was known as Sheff Wragg for many years – Scouse and Brummy are indicative of the lad's home town. Other names like Moppy (as Sir Gordon Richards was known because of his shock of thick dark hair), Ginger, Darkie, Snowy, Spider and Smiler derive from their appearances and mannerisms. Rabbit, presumably, was rather nervous during his early days in stables.

One of the greatest honours that lads could confer upon one of their fellows was to give him the name of a great horse that he had done. Until not so long ago there lived at the Glanely Rest at Exning an old man called Mahoney. His real name was Jack, but everybody called him Pretty Polly Mahoney as a tribute to his having done the great filly who won the 1,000 Guineas, the Oaks and the St Leger in 1904.

Pretty Polly was trained in the well-appointed Clarehaven Stables, where Jeremy Hindley has his horses today. That establishment stands a few yards farther up the Bury Road from the Freemason Lodge yard, and was built by Pretty Polly's trainer Peter Purcell Gilpin in 1901. He belonged to the old school of Newmarket trainers, who used to take a shotgun to the touts. Nowadays trainers co-operate with newspaper correspondents in keeping the public informed about the horses, mindful of the fact that public patronage of the racecourse and the betting shops is essential to the well-being of the racing industry.

Another unpleasant practice of the olden days was subjecting lads to gruesome initiation ceremonies when they were given their stable names. That sort of thing was stamped out long ago, but I must admit I have heard of apprentices being sent down to Gilbert's to buy a left-handed whip and glass spurs.

As I have said earlier, the lads at Warren Place are good all-round stablemen, but nevertheless most of them excel in one particular aspect of horsemanship. Some are at their best breaking yearlings, others at riding robust, boisterous colts, or handling highly strung fillies, riding very strong headstrong horses, or coaxing back to form horses that have become sour and ungenerous. One of my jobs as a trainer is to allot a horse to the care of the lad who is right for it, and similarly to ensure that the horses are ridden at exercise by the lads whose talents are of most use to them.

One of the Warren Place lads to have put a specialist talent to particularly good use during recent seasons is Yarmouth. He rides out at about ten stone, and has won the stable lads' heavyweight boxing title every year since 1977, but his kindness and patience with difficult horses have to be seen to be believed. When the one-time Derby hope Critique came to us from Ireland in the summer of 1981 he was said to be an awkward and unpleasant individual. He lived up to that reputation only too well, until he began to respond to Yarmouth, as though suddenly realizing that he was not without a friend in the world after all.

Whenever Critique became mulish or dug his toes in Yarmouth just talked to him, patted him, and generally made a fuss of him, until he did what was required, rather than giving him a backhander, or a few kicks up the rib. So quickly was Critique induced into a more amenable state of mind that he won at Kempton Park towards the end of August the first time we ran him. Next time out he was a winner again at Nottingham and a little more than a fortnight later he completed the hat-trick in the £12,000 Cumberland Lodge Stakes at Ascot. We kept him in the yard as a four-year-old in 1982, and he rewarded us by winning more than £36,000 in prize money through his successes in the Hardwicke Stakes at Royal Ascot and the September Stakes at Kempton Park.

Yarmouth has just got married. I did up one of the cottages next to the yard for him, and, needless to say, Critique's owner, Garo Vanian, has made a substantial contribution towards enabling him to set up home.

Before settling down to marriage Yarmouth was involved in more than one controversy, and I suspect he holds the record for paying for the most expensive Chinese meal of all time. He had a slight misunderstanding with another customer at the local takeaway, and in the mêlée that followed two lots of Chow Mein flew through a large plate-glass window. The result of that lively altercation was that the bill for the meal was about £350.

The Newbury Spring meeting in early April is our first 'away match' of the season, and the staff have been known to become over-exuberant on the trip. A few years ago Yarmouth was so full of high spirits – probably Gordons – that he appeared unable to lead his horse round the pre-parade ring. I was really annoyed, as these things never look good, and do nothing to improve the image of the stable. While in the saddling box I let him know my views in no uncertain terms, and physically threw him out of the door. Julie, who was standing near-by with one of our senior owners not noted for his sense of humour, said his exit from the box was quite spectacular. Another to be impressed was one of Ian Balding's lads, who told Ian's wife Emma about it.

'That's nothing,' observed Mrs Balding. 'Henry's father-in-law used to do it to his owners.'

I hasten to add that he did not, although he must have been sorely tempted once or twice.

In Willie Jardine – who is Scottish-born like myself – and Willie Jarvis I have two efficient assistant trainers. Both are excellent stablemen, and have ridden as amateurs on the flat. William Jarvis won on his first mount in public, Chance Belle at Redcar in 1977, and comes from Newmarket's oldest training family. One of his ancestors sent out Gustavus to become the first grey horse to win the Derby back in 1821, while his great-grandfather Bill Jarvis trained that great horse Cyllene, winner of the

Ascot Gold Cup in 1899 and an immensely influential sire from whom many of the best horses of recent years descend in tail-male line through Nearco. Bill Jarvis had three sons, William, Jack (later Sir Jack) and Basil, all of whom trained successfully at Newmarket.

William, the eldest, whose grandson and namesake is my assistant, trained for King George VI and other owners at Egerton House until he was forced into retirement by ill-health and the royal horses were transferred to Uncle Cecil. Ryan Jarvis, son of the royal trainer, turned out that splendid sprinter Absalom, and Lomond, Front Row and a lot of other good winners from the Phantom House stable before retiring in 1979. He is the father of Willie, who will eventually train at Phantom House, which is at present tenanted by that increasingly successful young trainer Willie Musson.

My travelling head lads are George Winsor and Frank Conlon. It is their duty to supervise the transport of the horses from the stable to the racecourse, and as they have to ensure every possible precaution is taken against our runners being nobbled while away from the yard, theirs is a most responsible job. They make the final declaration to run to the clerk of the course three-quarters of an hour before the race, and, with the help of their wives, always produce the owner's racing silks washed and pressed.

Frank Conlon is another member of a racing family. Both his father and his uncle were successful jockeys in Ireland. While apprenticed to Bob Ward he rode a useful sort of horse called Amos (subsequent winner of the Royal Hunt Cup) in public. He has as good a wit as any lad I know, and a fund of stories, most of which are quite unrepeatable.

The trial jockeys at Warren Place are Willie Snaith and Frank Storey, two tough little men who can always be relied upon to tell you a lot about their horses after they have ridden a bit of fast work. Willie Snaith began his career as an apprentice to Sam Armstrong at Middleham, and accompanied him to Warren Place, so he is no stranger to the stable. Subsequently he became a top-class light-weight. A very active rider, he would often push his mounts along almost from the start. Because he could always be seen to be trying so hard to win, he was very popular with the public, who called him 'The Pocket Hercules'. Among the races that he won for the Captain were the Chester Vase on Alcide in 1958 and the Great Metropolitan on Little Buskins in 1961, while for Sir Noel he won the Sussex Stakes on the Queen's Landau at Goodwood in 1954 and other races. I often wish that all the men I have had to ride for me were as cheerful and good-natured as Willie.

Frank Storey served his apprenticeship with George Colling. He has just started racing greyhounds, and many a morning at first lot he has the most wonderful reasons to account for the failure of the good thing of the previous night. Thinking back to the days of Dardanus, I can sympathize with him!

Woody was another marvellous work rider that we had. He was an Irishman, who had worked for Sir Noel for many years, and it was a shame that drink was a problem for him. It accounted for his having a number of jobs interspersed between his frequent returns to us. He was one of the best judges of a horse I have ever known. It was a sad day when he died in the summer of 1981, after not having had a drink for some considerable time. I still miss him.

Dodger Hooper, who worked for the Captain for a great number of years, is second head lad and in charge of the fillies' yard. Sid Harris, who drives the horsebox, was also with my stepfather. He is married to the daughter of my mother-in-law's cook, which makes a nice family attachment.

There is no better head lad than Paddy Rudkin. He is

unusually well-built for a stableman, and although he never stands still for a minute and is in charge of the breaking of nearly a hundred yearlings a season, his shadow never lessens. Much to the amusement of Julie and Alma – one of the girls, and a great friend of hers – he once appeared in a pair of new light-tan jodhpurs given to him by Peter Golding, whose famous Newmarket shop specializes in riding clothes, to try out a new line. Paddy insisted that they be given to him because he claims to be the only man in the town with a perfect figure. Nevertheless, there was much speculation in the yard as to who could have possibly ordered them in the first place, or whether Mr Golding had muddled up his inches with centimetres.

Jim White is the veteran of the stable. He was Sir Noel's travelling head lad for forty years, and still lives in his house at Warren Place. As well as looking after the chickens, he gets my hack ready in the morning. He is wonderful with his hands, and his hobby of making wooden toys and model farmyards ensures his great popularity with everybody's children. Jim is always lamenting that things are not done the way they used to be, and I am sure they are not, but there is simply not the time and the staff to make the old ways practicable any more.

The working grounds on the Newmarket Heath stretch out to the east and to the west of the town. Warren Place is on the eastern side – or Bury Side as it is called, as the road through it leads to Bury St Edmunds. It is on that part of the Heath nearest us, Warren Hill, that our horses come back into work in the late winter. Long, steady canters up the steep gradients of the hill put condition on to them and strengthen the leg muscles before they graduate to longer, faster work on the flat ground on Waterhall. The string has a long walk back from Waterhall, and it is not always pleasant. East Anglia in March can feel like the Arctic when the wind blows from the steppes of Russia unchecked by a mountain range.

At the end of March we begin using the gallops on the Racecourse Side, where, as implied by its name, both the Rowley Mile and the July courses are to be found. There is always something exciting about pulling out of the yard for the first visit of the year to the Racecourse Side, and seeing horses stretched out in an almost straight line for two miles or more as a result of gaps that have been cut in the Devil's Dyke.

The Devil's Dyke, which runs right across the Racecourse Side gallops, is an ancient fortification of unknown origin that stretches out for eight miles to the little Suffolk village of Reach. It could conceivably have been built by the Iceni, the ancient British tribe whom Queen Boadicea led in rebellion against the Romans in AD 60. A small blue flower that I have never seen anywhere else flourishes on the Devil's Dyke, and the story goes that it only grows on ground over which much blood has been spilt. Presumably, therefore, there was a great deal of fighting on this great earthwork in Roman times, or still earlier in our history.

The Racecourse Side gallops are rather too far from Warren Place for us to use them with any regularity, and once the horses are fit they do most of their work nearer home. On Bury Side we have the Limekilns, perhaps the most famous gallops in the world, Railway Land, Waterhall, New Ground, which is right opposite Warren Place, Side Hill, to the right of Warren Hill, and Long Hill, across the Moulton Road from Warren Hill, as well as various other working grounds.

When Newmarket was very much out of fashion among owners and trainers in the middle of the last century Jim Godding – whose daughter Norah married Cyllene's trainer Bill Jarvis – declared that if he could not train his Derby horse Macaroni on the Limekilns he could not train him anywhere. News of Macaroni having won the Derby of 1863 was greeted by the ringing of the bells of All Saints

Church to signal the salvation of Newmarket's reputation as a training centre. The going on the Limekilns never becomes firm, and they are only open when the rest of the gallops are too hard for use, but the slightest shower of rain makes the going on them soft, and they are closed immediately. Like the rest of the Heath, the Limekilns are owned by the Jockey Club, and use of them, or any other gallop, when they have been closed by the Jockey Club's agent, Robert Fellowes, incurs a heavy fine for the trainer. The long gallop on the Limekilns starts on Waterhall, and the foundations of the careers of many of the good horses featuring in the next chapter have been laid while they worked over that lovely stretch of ground.

I have far too much with which to busy myself without betting, and never do bet, but Julie is in a syndicate with a few of our lads. They have a couple of doubles and trebles a week, and after the stable had won 111 races in 1982 I was expecting a present from the punters. Julie was too embarrassed to reveal the profit, but I am reliably informed they cleared £8.72 over the season. So much for inside information.

# 6
## *The Champions*

We have been fortunate enough to have had many charming and high-class horses through our hands over the years. They are regarded as friends, as well as having been instrumental in keeping up our livelihood. It is not possible to include every one, but I would like to dedicate this chapter to all the horses – good and not so good – who have carried the Cecil banner in their various fields of endeavour. Many of the less talented horses have done their best, and you cannot ask for more. To them I say: 'You may be missing from this text, but in our hearts and minds you are not forgotten.'

**Bolkonski**

Luca Cumani was my assistant in 1975, and his father trained for Bolkonski's owner Carlo d'Alessio, a Roman lawyer, in Italy. Bolkonski was champion two-year-old in Italy the previous season, and in a bid to raise his value it was decided to send him over to us to train as a three-year-old.

He was a highly strung colt with a bad mouth. He hung to the right in his work, and this was a trait we never really eradicated. Fortunately, though, it was not so pronounced on the racecourse. He would pull hard, taking a lot out of himself, and was difficult to keep at his peak for very long. Those were his bad points. The good points are in the racing history books, which show how he achieved much to establish him as a truly top-class animal.

His first race as a three-year-old was the Craven Stakes, at Newmarket, where he ran a very good second to Louis Freedman's colt No Alimony, trained by Peter Walwyn, despite not being fully fit and tuned up. Considering he was up against a very fit horse, we were delighted with his performance, although the owner took some convincing to be brought to the same frame of mind.

Bolkonski's next race was to be the 2,000 Guineas, and although the preliminaries to this great race were a real nightmare, the result was glorious. We, unfortunately, had a stable lads' strike at the time, and not only were we operating the yard with a skeleton staff, we also had to overcome the picketing outside the stable gates. We had a goat to help keep the boys on the picket line amused. We were lucky to have the help of a number of amateurs in the yard, some mucking out and others riding. Some of them worked well, others were an absolute disaster. But thanks to them all we managed to get the horses out and exercised. The few horses in work were ridden by the nucleus of staff who remained. In some ways it was an exciting time, providing a real challenge. Looking back on it, and the calamity it could so easily have been, we always think of Wollow, who was to be the best of his generation as both a juvenile and a three-year-old. During the strike he was ridden out by an extremely heavy farmer who although nice and quiet was inclined to give the wretched colt a sore back.

Bolkonski's last gallop before the 2,000 Guineas told us he had to run very well. The gallop was paced by Peter Prompt, whose four wins in the previous season included a good race at Goodwood, and a decent four-year-old colt called Deerslayer, who in this particular exercise was ridden by Frankie Durr. The Italian jockey Franco Dettori had flown over to ride Bolkonski.

Peter Prompt and then Deerslayer led a very fast gallop over seven furlongs on Racecourse Side, and it was at the six-furlong post that Bolkonski picked them up easily and finished two or three lengths in front. On the night before the race the strikers dug a trench across the course near

A lovely view of Crathes Castle . . . it was a children's paradise

My mother and Uncle Cecil with, from top of slide, Bow, Jamie, me, David and Arthur

Freemason Lodge

Bolkonski, with Franco Dettori in the saddle, in the parade ring before landing my first classic success in the 1975 2000 Guineas

The house, Warren Place

One in a Million with Joe Mercer up. She is the fastest I have trained

Kris and Joe Mercer on their way to victory in the Sussex Stakes at Goodwood in 1980

Joe Mercer has victory in his sights on Light Cavalry in the 1980 St Leger

Le Moss beats Ardross in the Gold Cup at Goodwood in 1980

Lester Piggott rode his four-thousandth winner on Ardross in the Geoffrey Freer Stakes at Newbury in 1982. No wonder he is all smiles as he pats the great stayer

Parting of the ways . . . Lester and me at Newmarket

My head man Paddy Rudkin supervises work in the yard

Steve Cauthen joins us as stable jockey in 1985

With my wife Julie, our children Noel and Katie, and the dogs – Buckskin and Nancy

the start. It was an action which could only be looked upon with sadness and horror. The Rowley Mile course at Newmarket has been there for centuries, and that hallowed turf holds many great historical memories. So many champions had graced it, and now this. It is not very different from a vandal slashing an Old Master's picture of immense national value.

The big race was started by flag in front of the devastation, making it a few yards shorter than normal. Grundy, the champion two-year-old who was later to win the Derby and the King George VI and Queen Elizabeth Stakes, was the obvious favourite. Coming into the dip, Dettori set sail for home and took a two- or three-length lead which Grundy could never peg back. Bolkonski won by half a length. I had told Dettori that it was essential to get his horse really balanced running down the hill, to give a little more momentum with which to master the rising ground approaching the winning post. He rode the Newmarket course really well, and was to prove his prowess again in the 2,000 Guineas of the following year. Franco was a truly professional jockey, very short-legged and strong, and he could really use his stick. Horses ran very well for him. When he wanted that final burst he would pull his stick through most stylishly, give them a sharp slap down the shoulder . . . and away.

Back at the yard the echo of the mash buckets told us that the staff were feeding the horses. Carlo d'Alessio and Franco came back to Marriott with us, and, feeding-time over, the staff joined us at the entrance part of the building, where we all enjoyed a tremendous party. There is only one way to celebrate such a success, and that is with champagne. But in all the post-race hubbub it had slipped my mind that our supply at Marriott had run dry. Fortunately Jeremy Hindley was well stocked up, and sent over a crate. Morale was sky-high. It was our first classic win in England, and you cannot imagine how fantastic I felt. One of my most exciting thoughts was: 'What will the papers have to say tomorrow?' Good publicity is a great boon to a trainer with his thoughts on the future and new owners, with better horses.

Bolkonski went on to win the St James's Palace Stakes at Royal Ascot in breathtaking style, and then the Sussex Stakes at Goodwood. Being a rather free horse, he did not last until the end of the season, and was sold as a stallion to stand in France.

There was one incident involving Bolkonski which never fails to make me smile every time I think about it. We had had a poor winter and the horses had taken time to come to themselves. But one cannot force things, and in such circumstances one just has to wait. Up until the 2,000 Guineas we had managed only five minor winners, while other trainers were having more marked successes. A certain owner reckoned that there was something drastically wrong and that we had a virus or something in the yard. He sent an old ex-trainer who had a great reputation for having homoeopathic powers to check the horses. The man moved around the yard, putting his grubby fingers into the animals' eyes to check the pigment.

'This one's all wrong. It will take three weeks of treatment to get him right,' he said of one.

And of the next: 'He's even worse. Four weeks for him.'

I soon tired of this charade and, feeling the man was a crank, I put Bolkonski into the line for inspection.

'He's all wrong,' said the old man. 'I reckon he will be out of action for six weeks.'

'Strange that,' I told him. 'He must have caught the dreaded lurgy and deteriorated very quickly.'

He nodded knowingly.

'He won the 2,000 Guineas yesterday!' I laughed.

But I was pretty soon to have another battle on my

hands – with the lad who looked after Bolkonski. His name was Tom Dickie, a twenty-eight-year-old man who had joined the striking stable lads and was carried shoulder-high in front of the grandstand after the horse had won. In no way could I pay him the £1,000 he would normally have received as the lad who 'does' the winning horse.

**Wolver Hollow**

We owe so much to this big bay horse, as he was our first Group One winner. In fact, our first Group race winner of any description. In one's first year a victory like that of Wolver Hollow's in the Eclipse can really put one on the map. People begin to notice you, and to talk to you. Uncle Cecil, who bought Wolver Hollow for 4,000 guineas as a yearling at Newmarket, was eventually left the horse by Mrs Iselin. She was 101, and still owned the horse, when he won the Eclipse, but unfortunately she was in a coma, never knew of his great achievement, and died soon afterwards.

Uncle Cecil had trained the horse until his retirement, and managed him for Mrs Iselin when I took the reins. I think that as Uncle Cecil's training career was drawing to an end, Wolver Hollow's three-year-old campaign was harder than it would otherwise have been. The horse was tall, and on the weak side, and I felt that he needed time. He had wound up his two-year-old campaign by finishing a close fourth to Dart Board in the Dewhurst, and reappeared in the Greenham to finish third, beaten a neck and a head, to Play High and Reform.

He was slowly into his stride and finished in the ruck in Royal Palace's 2,000 Guineas, but he seemed to be wandering about a lot under Doug Smith, and was very unbalanced. After finishing fourth to Reform in the St James's Palace Stakes at Royal Ascot he won his maiden very easily at Newcastle, followed up by winning again at

York, and later ran a terrific race in the Cambridgeshire to finish third of thirty-four behind Lacquer.

He had not really made a tremendous impact on the racing scene, but we looked forward to better things to come in his four-year-old career. It almost never materialized. Between his second and third season he developed grass sickness (the cause of this equine disease is not known) and very nearly died, spending the best part of a year turned out at Barton Stud near Bury St Edmunds. We used to drive Uncle Cecil over every week to see the horse, and what a pitiful sight it was to behold. Wolver Hollow was never a robust colt, but now he stood with his head down and was hardly able to muster the strength to raise it. He was just skin and bone, with muscles so slack that even his lower lip drooped down, while his backbone stood up. He had no quarters, and the most terrible poverty lines.

The car was like a morgue on the drive home. No one uttered a word, after so dreadful a sight. Then one day we noticed he was far more attentive and interested in what was going on around him. As I closed the paddock gate behind me he looked up. Painfully and very slowly, he walked up to us. I held in front of him a handful of dandelions I had picked, and he nibbled at them. It was then that I knew he would recover. We got him back on to the racecourse in August, when we went to Deauville and finished fourth in the Prix Gontaut Biron. Nine days later he won the Prix Ridgeway on the same course. He followed up by being second to Paddy Prendergast's World Cup in the Queen Elizabeth II Stakes at Ascot before running another fine race in the Cambridgeshire, going down a neck to Emerilo, to whom he was conceding 27lb, in a field of thirty-five.

As a five-year-old he made up into a beautiful horse. He worked extremely well, and everybody including Uncle Cecil became very excited about his prospects. His comeback was in the Jubilee Stakes at Kempton, and he turned in a truly fantastic performance under top weight to be second to Sovereign Ruler, conceding no less than 35lb. Jimmy Lindley was his new jockey, and he often drove to Newmarket to ride him on the Heath. His final gallop before the Lockinge Stakes at Newbury was absolutely devastating. Tower Walk, trained by Geoffrey Barling, was the favourite, and it was arranged that we should work with him. Stan Smith rode Wolver Hollow, and I told him not to be too hard on the horse, as Tower Walk would probably run him off his feet. I wanted Stan just to sit in behind and let the horse enjoy himself. The rider did this perfectly, and as they approached the rising ground and the final furlong Wolver Hollow was just cantering. Stan let him have a little rein, and he went past Tower Walk and his lead horse as if they were standing still to finish five lengths in front. Wherever Tower Walk finished in the race Wolver Hollow should be at least five lengths in front. It was not to be. Wolver Hollow showed no enthusiasm at all, and finished last of six to Habitat, beaten by some twenty lengths. Tower Walk was second. I felt absolutely useless, and my confidence absolutely shattered.

Perhaps an easy race in a handicap would give the horse a little confidence, I thought. Uncle Cecil had said that I had to train him for the Eclipse, but the very idea filled me with horror. I thought it completely idiotic, and went to Sandown on Eclipse day only because I had to. Julie felt terribly sorry for me, and I am sure she was pleased that she was not going to be involved in what on the face of it was a fruitless exercise, even though Wolver Hollow had finished second to Connaught in the Prince of Wales's Stakes at Royal Ascot. Lester Piggott had left no stone unturned in an attempt to get on the favourite Park Top, trained by Bernard Van Cutsem. Having failed to secure the ride on her, he reluctantly climbed up on Wolver Hollow.

They went a good gallop, and Piggott was sitting out at

the back coming into the straight. Then he crept up on the inside rail turning for home, took the lead a furlong and a half out and held off the challenge of Park Top to win by two and a half lengths. Park Top came very late, and many people said she was unlucky. I do not agree. I honestly believe nothing would have beaten my old horse that day. It was a beautiful piece of riding by Piggott, and highlighted an absolutely thrilling day. From being a nobody I was suddenly being introduced to all and sundry. They thought I was wonderful. We have a painting of Wolver Hollow in the dining-room at Warren Place, and his shoes are on onyx ash trays. He was to sire Wollow, who in the not too distant future was to give us so much fun and satisfaction, and to bring us everlasting memories.

**Parthenon and Relay Race**

When Sir Gordon Richards retired from training in 1969 he had in his care a three-year-old stayer called Parthenon, who had completed a hat-trick before running a tremendous race to be sixth in the Cesarewitch, which does not favour horses in only their second season because of its severity. The horse was owned by Sir Reginald Macdonald-Buchanan, who at the time had horses with Sir Noel. My father-in-law when offered the horse to train suggested to Sir Reginald that we would love to have him. Sir Noel was fairly full, and did not particularly want to train a stayer.

Parthenon was a great big brown gelding with a narrow ribcage, a plain, almost Roman head and large soup-plate feet. He was a lovely character and a real gentleman, just like his owner. He had a long, devouring stride and was an out-and-out galloper. Greville Starkey was my stable jockey at the time, and they got on terribly well. Greville's great judgment of pace was essential to the success of Parthenon, for one needed a true gallop for a horse like him, and he often had to make his own running. His three-length victory in the Queen Alexandra Stakes in 1970 was our first Royal Ascot success, and made for an exhilarating day. He went on to win the Goodwood Cup, leading from start to finish, and later finished third, beaten less than two lengths, in the Prix Gladiateur at Longchamp. Parthenon liked some give in the ground, and I remember old Sir Reginald being worried that the ground at Longchamp would be too firm. I could not understand his thinking, because the previous day the going had been perfect. It turned out that Sir Reginald, bothered and excited about the race, had got up early on the morning of the event and was seen pacing up and down under the enormous cedar-tree, digging his heels in and shaking his head. That patch of ground had, of course, never encountered the rain!

I have coupled Relay Race with Parthenon as they were the two best horses we had for Sir Reginald. Relay Race was a black colt with a white blaze. He was narrow and very inclined to get jarred up. This tendency was enough to prevent him from coming up a true good horse, and he was never able to realize his full potential.

As a three-year-old in 1973 he won his maiden by five lengths at Newmarket and then a handicap at Doncaster. He was very unlucky in running in the Dante Stakes at York, where he was shut in and came too late, going down by a short head to Owen Dudley. Once or twice Greville managed to get shut in on him and then pulled him out too sharply when an opening came. This was inclined to jar the horse. I retired him for the season after he finished sixth to Morston in the 1973 Derby. He ran in the Derby in blinkers, because he had become slightly jarred up and reluctant. Falling down the hill at Epsom, he was last into the straight. But he made up a tremendous amount of ground to finish as close as he did.

It was after the John Porter Stakes, his first race of 1974 when he was a fast finishing third to Freefoot, that I decided to let Lester Piggott try the horse, and Greville made the decision to go freelance.

In early May Relay Race won the Jockey Club Stakes at Newmarket very easily, and then on Sir Noel's advice I put him away for the Hardwicke Stakes at Ascot. Sometimes when you ease horses off they do not always come back. This was the case with Relay Race. He did win the Hardwicke Stakes by half a length, but he was not the same horse that ran at Newmarket. Looking back on Relay Race's career, his moodiness and reluctance must be put down to the wretched horse feeling his shoulders. If I were training him today I am sure I would not pull him out on to a racecourse in the circumstances that I did on one or two occasions.

In July 1974 he ran in the Grand Prix de Saint-Cloud, and I think was favourite. He had been working very well, and we were hopeful that he would win. Sir Reginald, Julie, myself and Charles Rowe – who is my solicitor, and a great friend – flew over to France in a small chartered plane and had a rather heavy lunch. In France when you saddle your horse you put the number cloth underneath the weight cloth, whereas in England it is done the other way round. I of course did it the English way. Down at the start Piggott dismounted and resaddled Relay Race – after a great deal of effort. As he tried to put the saddle back on, the horse ran round in circles, pulling off both his hind shoes. After this fiasco he finished well down the field.

Sir Reginald rushed down, with the rest of us, bewildered, following. He wanted to hear what Piggott had to say.

'Piggott, what happened?' shouted Sir Reginald, slightly flushed after the wine at lunch.

Lester turned to me and said, 'The trouble with you is that you couldn't put a saddle between the two humps of a b----- camel.'

Sir Reginald, who was as deaf as a door-post, turned to Julie and asked, 'What did Piggott say?'

'He said the horse did not run very well, Sir Reginald,' Julie lied.

'Oh, never mind,' was the reply. And we all set off to get a taxi and a plane home.

**Wollow**

Wollow, a bay colt by Wolver Hollow, was a two-year-old in the year Bolkonski won the Guineas, 1975, and was to continue the wonderful run of luck enjoyed by Carlo d'Alessio. He was bred by my half-brother, Arthur Boyd-Rochfort, at the Tally Ho Stud in Ireland, and came from that wonderful Black Ray family, the family of the great Mill Reef. Arthur was always very keen on him, and told me to have a really good look at him when he arrived at the sale paddocks in Newmarket. He was a light colt, tall and leggy, and always very much on the narrow side. To balance out these faults he was a very good walker, had a lot of class about the head and tremendous presence.

I badly wanted to buy the colt, and not at that time being in a financial position to buy on spec, I looked around for an owner. Charles St George was the obvious choice, but after he brought in a heart specialist he spurned the colt when it was revealed that he had a murmur.

I persuaded Mr d'Alessio to buy him, and was most satisfied when we secured him, with only a few bids, at 7,000 guineas. I have always felt sorry for Arthur, the vendor, who thought the world of him, and had expected a lot more.

Wollow started to work very well the following July, and Mr d'Alessio had another colt called Take Your Place, who was equally promising. Take Your Place went on to win the Futurity and was second top-rated two-year-old behind Wollow in the Free Handicap. Unfortunately, he developed a wind problem, and never fulfilled his promise. Both he and Wollow made their debuts over a two-day July meeting at Newmarket, and each won convincingly. Wollow's next outing was the Fitzroy House Stakes at headquarters, which he won without being extended, and he went on to win the Champagne Stakes at Doncaster.

Vincent O'Brien had at the time a very highly rated colt called Malinowski, who had just won by ten lengths at the Curragh. He was the top Irish two-year-old, and came over to take on Wollow in the Dewhurst. Wollow won well, and went into the winter as favourite for both the 2,000 Guineas and the Derby.

He wintered well, and won the Greenham very impressively. He had a terrific turn of foot, and won many of his races coming off the pace. His homework was a joy to watch. He really was a lovely colt to train. I always think that the best horses have one thing in common. When working across the flat on Racecourse Side they go straight up to the winning post. I watch them coming towards me from the end of the gallop, having usually put the star at the back of a group of four or five horses. The idea is for them to draw upsides two furlongs out and then accelerate. The really good horse does this so quickly. One second he is settled at the back of the pack and the next he is easing up two lengths in front. I am not saying they are faster than light, but they quicken so well that one barely sees them pass their working partners.

Wollow won the 2,000 Guineas by accelerating smoothly to take up the running in the final furlong. The next step was the Derby. It was lovely to have won the 2,000 Guineas two years in succession, and for a long time I was thinking I might complete the treble in it. I hoped that when Sir Noel retired his American owners, the Popes, might leave me J. O. Tobin, who would definitely have won the 2,000 Guineas in 1977. But it was not to be. The colt was sent back to America.

Wollow lined up for the Derby hot favourite, with

Franco Dettori having had his first ride on the course on our thirteen-times winner Fools Mate in an earlier race on the card. That had been a disaster. He managed to get himself closed in on the rails, and was never seen with a chance. My Derby confidence had sunk to a low ebb. I had the feeling that this was not going to be our day.

Wollow did not get the best of rides, or runs, although I do not entirely blame his jockey because the horse failed to get the trip. He finished fifth to Empery, but never really got into a challenging position. Wollow was really a miler, and was never beaten over that distance. Many horses do not come bouncing back after having experienced a defeat like that. Wollow did. He won the Eclipse on the disqualification of the French colt Trepan, who was found to have traces of caffeine in his blood. It is my opinion that Wollow would never have beaten Trepan that day. Trepan was a stronger horse then, and I feel a race like the Eclipse favours the older horses at that time of the year. The three-year-olds only come into their own around King George VI and Queen Elizabeth time.

Wollow went on to win the Benson and Hedges at York over one mile two and a half furlongs from Crow after easily winning the Sussex Stakes at Goodwood. I withdrew him from the King George because the heavy rain had made the ground like a mud bath. He went over the top in the Champion Stakes, and was never going well behind Vitiges.

Wollow was a great horse, and I would nominate him as about the best youngster I have been fortunate enough to have had through my hands. Perhaps, being slight and immature, he did not quite last out his second season, as we were trying to put what would have been the main races of his four-year-old career into his three-year-old campaign.There is no mistaking that he was a very high-class colt, and it is sad that after such a short career at stud in England he was condemned and sold to Japan.

**Falkland**

When Jack Waugh retired from training in the famous Heath House stable – once part of the larger one to which Fred Archer was attached throughout most of his incredible career – he had some dozen horses belonging to Lord Howard de Walden. I was thrilled when Lord Howard asked me to train for him, though I had only enough boxes for the two-year-olds and two of the older horses. Of the latter we took a good little filly called Benita, who was to win us two races, despite being susceptible to becoming jarred up, and were then left with the choice between the colts Lanzarote and Falkland. Having heard of Lanzarote's hard race in blinkers at Yarmouth, I felt that Falkland had the greater potential. In due course Lanzarote made up into a top-class National Hunt horse. But that would have been no good to me!

Falkland too turned out be really good. A great big, nearly black horse, he had a rather high knee action. He had run twice as a two-year-old, giving every indication of being useful on the second of these outings when second of thirty-six in a one-mile Newmarket maiden. Falkland stayed well, although he did not possess a great turn of foot. But once put through the gears, he could really gallop. It was a case of going through the motions gradually to get that top gear, and once there, he was a difficult horse to beat.

As a three-year-old in 1971 he won his maiden at Newmarket in the April, and followed up with an easy win in a maidens-at-closing at the Guineas meeting in May. He then went to Sandown, where he won the Richmond Handicap by four lengths. As he went on improving we decided to run him in the St Leger, and as an outsider he very nearly won it. In a blanket finish he was third, beaten a neck and a head, to a tough campaigner called Athens Wood, trained by Tom Jones. He led from start to finish, and I feel that if the pace had been stronger we might have won. But it was not. We could have gone on coming into the straight. But we did not.

Falkland easily won the Queen's Vase at Ascot as a four-year-old, and then hacked up on the Princess of Wales's Stakes at Newmarket. Unfortunately, he went in a tendon soon afterwards, otherwise he would have made a fantastic Cup horse the following year. He took a long time to get his strength, and one and a half miles was really slightly too short for him. He broke down probably due to his action, as he was inclined to hit the ground very hard. If he had stayed sound he would have made one of the best Ascot Gold Cup winners for years, of that I have no doubt, because he was a very high-class horse. When favourite for the 1972 Ebor Handicap, his last race, he panicked after the horse in the next stall misbehaved and hit his head on the front of the stalls, concussing himself. He fell out like a drunk, and trailed round near the rear of the field. He would never go into stalls again. Once those old horses have lost their nerve one really has to call it a day.

**Roussalka**

At the Houghton Sales in 1973 Captain Marcos Lemos and Nicky Phillips asked me to buy them a filly each. Nice fillies were few and far between that year, and after a long search we found only two we really liked. They both came from Dalham Hall Stud, one by Habitat, and the other by King Emperor, a Bold Ruler horse who was to turn out a complete disaster as a sire in Europe. Both owners were keen on the Habitat, but in the end we managed to allot the Habitat filly to Nicky, and the Captain took the other. It was just as well it worked out like that, for I would have lost Roussalka the following year, when the owner decided to have his horses trained privately by Clive Brittain. The filly I lost turned out to be very moderate, but the Habitat, although she did not have the best of hocks, trained to be about the best of her generation.

Given the name Roussalka, she was pretty temperamental, and once when I was showing her to some American people, one remarked how sweet she was. I assured the lady that this was not the case, and asked her lad, Billy Aldridge, to untie her. Roussalka let fly with both her back legs, just missing my hastily retreating guests. At the same time she came round with her head and tore off my new yellow Cashmere pullover. It was a rather expensive demonstration from the filly. Roussalka, a very tough bay filly with a marvellous set of quarters, was inclined to kick anything too close to her in the string.

She made her debut at Yarmouth, where she won unchallenged, and after being beaten by a neck in a maidens-at-closing at Ascot her next engagement was the Cherry Hinton Stakes at Newmarket. Unfortunately, she banged an eye, and could see very little on her left side. Hanging across the course from one side to the other, she still won by four lengths in a very fast time.

She won the Princess Margaret Stakes at Ascot, and then she went for a warm-up race at Kempton Park with the Cheveley Park Stakes in mind. She won the preparatory race, but rather unconvincingly, and the writing was on the wall. She was going over the top, and although she ran a fair fourth in the Cheveley Park she was well below her best.

Roussalka appeared to winter well, and we had high hopes that she would win the 1,000 Guineas. However, she showed little sparkle early on, and we had to abandon our Guineas plan completely, with the hope that she would come to herself in time for Ascot. We felt our way, but her work was unimpressive, and I began to wonder if she would ever come back. Just before Ascot we took her over to Racecourse Side and worked her with, among others, Bolkonski. She worked every bit as well as the 2,000 Guineas winner, if not slightly better, and they both went on to win at the Royal meeting. Then Roussalka went to Goodwood, our favourite racecourse, for the Nassau Stakes, which she won well. She became the first filly to win the Nassau twice when the following year the race became open to four-year-olds. She took a long time to come to herself that season, and it was her only success. She had tried to drop herself out in the straight, and looked like being last. But Piggott, in his most forceful fashion, managed to rouse her out of her sulkiness, and she got up to beat Sauceboat – who was trained by Julie's father – by half a length. She retired to stud in America, and although she has so far failed to produce anything of her own calibre I am sure it is only a matter of time before she does.

**Gunner B**

Gunner B was as tough as old boots, and had more character than almost all our other horses put together. He came to us from Geoff Toft at the advanced age of five. He had shown some good form in the past, but when winning an amateurs race at Newmarket on his last appearance but one of 1977 he had hung ominously. Having refused an offer for him, the owner decided a change of environment was needed, especially as Toft had little with which to work him, and he was sent to Warren Place.

There was nothing nasty about him, but he was a funny old thing, and we decided that to keep him sweet he should be allowed to get away with a lot and be shown a few concessions. To check him when he jibbed and fooled around might have soured him once and for all. He was a thick-set, medium-sized horse with a tough but attractive thick head. The more he thrived, the more attractive he seemed to become. Gunner B hated going into the canter, which meant that the retired travelling head man, Jim White, had to follow him every morning in the old stable van and gently persuade him. This involved Jim standing behind him and clapping and waving his arms until the horse decided that enough was enough. Paddy Rudkin rode him in all his routine daily exercise, and riding him was anything but straightforward. From time to time Gunner B would feel like having a bit of fun, and try his best to unseat his rider. But Paddy knew him so well that they invariably remained in partnership.

He wintered very well, and we decided that one and a quarter miles was probably his best trip. He came out at the Craven meeting at Newmarket, in the Earl of Sefton Stakes, and won nicely. Gunner B usually worked well, and would tell you when he was right and raring to go. I thought one more race before Ascot would be enough, and the Brigadier Gerard Stakes at Sandown was won on the way. He won the Prince of Wales's Stakes at Royal Ascot very easily, and was regarded as the most impressive winner of the meeting. He then went on to win the Eclipse, and ran fine races in the Benson and Hedges and the Champion Stakes. So many horses of Gunner B's age have been through a lot and have had enough, but he had not, and was tough and genuine until the end. He retired to stud in the north.

**One in a Million**

One In A Million is owned by Helena Springfield Ltd, and was the first horse owned by the company to win a classic. She was undoubtedly the fastest of either sex that I have trained.

After establishing herself as champion two-year-old filly of 1978 she went on to win the Nell Gwyn Stakes, the 1,000 Guineas and the Coronation Stakes at Royal Ascot the following season. She never really stayed a mile, but had put so much daylight between herself and the rest of the field two furlongs out at Newmarket that they could not peg her back in the 1,000 Guineas. A small, light filly and on the narrow side, she was, however, a true athlete.

**Hello Gorgeous**

Bought by Daniel Wildenstein for only 50,000 dollars, Hello Gorgeous was to prove nearly the best of his generation as a two-year-old in 1979. He was by Mr Prospector, a very popular stallion but inclined to throw slightly straight-legged horses. Hello Gorgeous inherited this trait. He arrived from America rather later than most of the other yearlings that year, and went into one of the two boxes in my yard nicknamed 'The Black Hole of Calcutta'. I had made them by converting two garages, and the only trouble was I forgot to put in any windows. But horses like Gunner B have done very well in them, so I have left them as they are.

Hello Gorgeous was a bright chestnut, and my first glimpse of him gave me the impression that he was a cheeky, colty horse and not to be trusted. I could not have been more wrong. Once in work he became a real gentleman, showing plenty of guts as well as ability. He was a slightly immature, unfurnished colt, and took a long time to acclimatize. He went back a lot in the spring, but then came along nicely enough, and in June I thought it would do him good to have a run. A York race was chosen, and he duly won. Although he did it readily in a field of nineteen, I felt that the race had taken a lot out of him, and it would be better to sit tight with him for a while.

After a time it occurred to me that the rest was not benefiting him at all. He had lost weight, getting rather lanky and scrawny, and I was not at all happy with him. But fortunately he suddenly began to thrive and gained weight all round. He seemed to be showing much more enthusiasm, and started to look as if he might be ready to run again. He won the Royal Lodge and the Futurity, and went into the winter very highly rated.

We had in the yard another fine two-year-old, a Hoist the Flag colt called Ginistrelli, who had hacked up in both his races when ridden by first Joe Mercer and then the American jockey Steve Cauthen. This colt had a tall reputation, and was clearly regarded as a 2,000 Guineas candidate. I had high hopes of him, and probably painted too bright a picture of his prowess, as is my habit. I am inclined to build up my geese into swans, and sometimes in the end everybody is disappointed. But on the other hand, there is an argument in favour of it. One has to be enthusiastic and put one's whole heart into a horse's career. By doing this one hopes to get the best out of him. To train a horse for the 2,000 Guineas, for example, is no fun and a pointless exercise unless you can convince yourself that there is a real live chance of winning.

Early in 1980 Hello Gorgeous was galloped with Ginistrelli. It was a foggy morning, but the sun was just beginning to break through the clouds. Newmarket had had little rain and the Limekilns were open. Charles St George, Ginistrelli's owner, came out to watch, and we decided to work the horses over seven furlongs straight. Hello Gorgeous – who was never going to be sharp enough to win the 2,000 Guineas – finished about six lengths in front. They had gone at a pretty good pace, without the riders murdering them, and the gallop clearly told us which path to take. Hello Gorgeous came out again in the Heathorn Stakes, at the Newmarket Guineas meeting – he had already confirmed he was no Guineas horse when only fifth to Final Straw in the Greenham – and ran Royal Fountain to a neck. He went on to beat Master Willie a neck in the Dante after a stirring battle throughout the final furlong, and was then strongly fancied for the Derby.

Ginistrelli had finished third, beaten two and a half lengths, to Henbit in the Sandown Classic Trial, and then won the Lingfield Derby Trial from a field that was less than moderate. He was retired after finishing third to Prince Bee in the Predominate Stakes at the Goodwood meeting, transferred to Kempton Park and sold to America as a stallion.

Because Hello Gorgeous was by Mr Prospector I had my reservations about whether he would stay the trip in the Derby. I felt that one and a quarter miles was far enough for him, but Daniel Wildenstein wanted the horse to take his chance. Joe Mercer had him beautifully poised coming into the straight, and moved up two and a half furlongs out with the eventual winner, Henbit, to within a length of the leader. But my worst fears were realized when it became apparent that Hello Gorgeous did not get the mile and half. In the final furlong he was going up and down on the spot, and finished sixth.

Although the Eclipse favours older horses, it was decided to run Hello Gorgeous against Ela-Mana-Mou. He turned in probably his best ever performance, going down by three-quarters of a length. I think he would have won if there had been overnight rain. He never really let himself go on firm ground, and having had two hard races on it, he was jarred up and never ran again. This was a great pity, because he was made hot favourite for the Benson and Hedges, which went to Master Willie. He was bought by the Coolmore Stud to stand in Ireland. He should be a great success.

**Le Moss**

If Le Moss were in a pack of cards, he would be a joker. In a comedy duo he would never play the straight man. This slightly tubular, narrow horse was a total enigma; stubborn as a mule and exasperating at home, but as honest as the day is long on a racecourse. He was quite extraordinary.

Levmoss won the 1969 Arc de Triomphe from Park Top after trotting up in the Ascot Gold Cup, and Le Moss – also bred at the Brownstown Stud in Ireland – was his full brother. Mr d'Alessio had given 26,000 guineas for him as a yearling, and my first impression on seeing him in Ireland was what a poor walker he was. But he had a certain something about him, and I agreed to take him on. He was so backward as a two-year-old that it was October before he saw a racecourse. His immaturity had made for a very trying time and so when he ran on to be seventh of twenty-four at Sandown we were delighted. He was already looking as though he might be capable of following in his brother's footsteps.

In May of the following year he won his maiden at Newmarket, and a month later went for the Queen's Vase at Royal Ascot, where he showed great resolution by battling on to get the better of Antler by a head in the last few strides. He went on to win at both Ayr and Goodwood in the tenacious style that was to become his hallmark, and then ran courageously again to be second to Julio Mariner in the St Leger.

Le Moss's Ascot Gold Cup victory of 1979 was tinged with sadness, for the horse he beat was Buckskin, a particular favourite of mine. We will come to him, and that race, later. Le Moss also won the Doncaster Cup and the Goodwood Cup, and lost no medals in being beaten by Totowah in the Jockey Club Cup at Newmarket. He had shown himself to be a stayer supreme, and I felt there was no reason why he should not clean up the Cups again in 1980. But things did not go at all according to plan. To begin with Le Moss was confined to his box for six weeks in the spring after pulling a muscle. And when he finally recovered work was the last thing on his mind.

All attempts to get him to gallop were met with a stonewall refusal. He would jib and stand completely still for a seeming eternity, with a look in his eye that said 'You must be bloody joking, mate' and he would not jump off. By this time I had too many horses in my care to be able to devote abnormal periods of time to an individual. He would be beaten a distance in a gallop with the maidens, and I had to use a bit of psychology on him, giving him the impression that I had reached the point where I had become so exasperated that I was ready to give up on him.

A lad called Alan Welbourn took Le Moss across the Heath, and they did long and lonely periods of exercise. I could see that Le Moss was revelling in this preferential treatment by the way he strutted around the place. But with Alan weighing in the region of ten and a half stone, he was doing more than he thought. I kidded him a bit in the evenings, too, for he was dispatched to the equine pool in Newmarket, where he was given enough work to make up for what he had missed during the day while he thought we were pandering to his whims. A preparatory race for the Ascot Gold Cup had long since been out of the question, and I decided instead to take him for a couple of racecourse spins. The cunning old devil seemed well aware we were out to hoodwink him, and proceeded to work atrociously at both Kempton and Yarmouth, where he struggled to stay with an old handicapper of mine called Francesco. He knew there was no race. He knew it was not for prize money.

The awful fear one has of horses with characters like Le Moss is that they might decide to loaf around during a race. I had nightmares about Gold Cup day, and when I arrived at Ascot I was still dreading that eventuality. Without the benefit of a previous outing I failed to see how he could possibly win this great race, but I should have known better! He led virtually from start to finish, shaking off challenge after challenge, and held on by three-quarters of a length from the last challenger of them all, Ardross. That success was probably the most satisfying I have ever had from a professional viewpoint. Le Moss went on to win the Goodwood Cup and the Doncaster Cup again before going down by half a length in the Prix Gladiateur at Longchamp, his last race before going back to Brownstown Stud to stand as a stallion.

**Buckskin**

I am reputed to have said that Buckskin is the best horse I have ever trained. That statement may have been made in the excitement of the moment after some great victory of his, but it is not far wrong.

Buckskin had a severe handicap. He had dropped soles to his feet, and had to wear built-up shoes. And as if that was not enough disadvantage for a horse, he had a very nasty suspensory ligament on his off-fore joint, necessitating his being put as long as four hours a day under the hosepipe. This soaking helped his circulation, and although the ligament was often very sore and like a balloon, he stood up to training right through until well into his sixth year, and even then did not completely break down. It has to be said that in his last race he was feeling those old legs badly, and would never have taken another outing.

Yelapa, once the champion two-year-old of France, sired Buckskin, whom many regarded as an out-and-out stayer, so that when finally retired to stud he became another in the long line of horses dismissed as long-distance specialists, and never given a chance as a stallion. As far as I am concerned, he was a very high-class middle-distance horse, and, I feel, did not really stay. But because of his legs one could not sharpen him up, and his work had to be long and gradual. It was one thing to ask him a question a few times a season on the racecourse, but to have done so frequently at home would almost certainly have broken him down. So the distances of his races were increased, and it was really only his class which saw him through in those which would have found out ordinary horses. Many horses develop 'character' as they grow older, rather like ageing gentlemen, and Buckskin was one of them. It was not uncommon for owners touring the yard to see a chicken flapping around the corner of a row of boxes, hotly pursued by Buckskin, with an eager twinkle lighting up his eyes. He had the run of the entire yard, and with his tremendous presence was a dominating figure. One got the feeling that everything in the yard revolved around him, like the wheels around the axle of a car.

Buckskin had in the first place been trained in France by Angel Penna, and then joined Peter Walwyn at Lambourn. When he came to us as a five-year-old in the middle of 1978 I was warned that hard ground would probably break him down, as after a great deal of racing his leg was really beginning to play him up. I decided to take a gamble. If the ground was to his liking, I thought, he would really let himself go, and do almost too much. However, if it was on the hard side, I reasoned, perhaps he would look after himself and do as little as was necessary. I kept him to firmish ground, and after running away with the Doncaster Cup he won the Jockey Club Cup in October to an ovation throughout the final furlong, for he had captured the hearts of all racing enthusiasts. Buckskin was kept in training as a six-year-old with only one race in mind, the two-and-a-half-mile Ascot Gold Cup. His preparatory race was the Henry II Stakes at Sandown, and he turned it into a procession, winning by fifteen lengths.

What followed at Ascot makes me feel like Judas Iscariot. Out of sentiment Joe Mercer had chosen to ride Buckskin in preference to Le Moss, and in the short straight they looked all over the winners. But Buckskin began to tire, and changed his legs. Lester Piggott had been pushing Le Moss along in the rear of the field, and eventually got a run out of him that brought him upsides Buckskin. It was now obvious that, despite Buckskin's efforts to fight off his stablemate, his poor legs would not match his mental enthusiasm. Seven lengths was Le Moss's winning margin, and although I saddled the first two it remains the saddest moment of my training career.

Buckskin finished a leg-weary horse. I hardly dared look him in the eye, for had his legs not needed all that cotton-wool and bandaging he was a horse who could have won a King George and an Arc de Triomphe.

**Kris**

Lord Howard de Walden's yearling colts in 1977 seemed so lacking in promise that his stud manager, Leslie Harrison, and I tried to persuade him to sell all five and reinvest in two more attractive prospects. The owner refused to entertain the idea, and how lucky for all of us he did!

Between them the colts won twenty-four races, and they included the greatest product of Lord Howard's stud up to that time, the champion miler Kris. Together with several of Lord Howard's yearlings, he was broken and ridden away by Bobby Jones and Jack Button at Wickhambrook, showing at even this early stage the good-humoured wilfulness and anxiety to get on with the job which he displayed at home throughout his career.

Kris made his racecourse debut in a maiden at Leicester in June. I desperately hoped he would win, because Lord Howard's horses at Warren Place were going through a lean patch. He obliged, winning by two lengths like a nice horse, then proceeded to clear the unsaddling enclosure with the most extraordinary display of over-excitement. Before his next race, some three weeks later, Kris gave the first indication that he might be something special. He went exceptionally well in a gallop with Main Reef, who a few days later won the Chesham Stakes at Royal Ascot by five lengths. It was hardly surprising, therefore, that he was untroubled to win at Folkestone, despite a 10lb penalty.

Kris pulled a muscle in his quarters not long afterwards, and I was unable to run him again until mid-October at York, where he earned his place in the Horris Hill Stakes, his only major engagement, by spreadeagling a useful field, and strode home eight lengths clear at the end of six furlongs. Over the additional furlong at Newbury Joe Mercer tried to restrain him, but Kris fought his rider very hard, and nearly brought about his own defeat. Having taken up the running two furlongs out, he was headed by Hardgreen, and it needed all Joe's tenacity to land him in front on the line. The next day Lord Howard married Gilly Mountgarret, and the Horris Hill Stakes made a suitable wedding present from Warren Place.

Kris continued to improve and strengthen through the winter, and following an easy success over Young Generation in the Greenham he became my main hope for the 2,000 Guineas, although I was also running Lyphard's Wish, who had beaten Tromos in the Craven Stakes.

A few days before the Guineas, Kris rapped his off-fore joint, and an apricot Yorkshire boot became an essential part of his equipment. All the same, I have never understood how he came to be beaten in the 2,000 Guineas, for I can find no obvious excuses. He was not well drawn, but the winner, Tap On Wood, was drawn right next to him. Having been ridden early on in the race to get a decent position, and then taken up the running a furlong from home, Kris had no answer to Tap On Wood's finishing speed, hard though he fought. It is regrettable that the two horses were never to meet again, for I am sure that Kris would have shown himself to be the better, especially later in the season. After the Guineas I let Kris down and earmarked the Heron Stakes at Kempton as a preparatory race for Royal Ascot. The Kempton event appeared to be a formality for him, but it was not without incident. As the field came into the straight the others all tacked over to the stands side, leaving Kris galloping towards a protruding section of the running rail. To avoid disaster Joe asked the horse to quicken as he scraped round the obstruction, leaning away like a cow-pony. Thanks to his agility, and considerable acceleration, an accident was averted and he won very easily, but not without having given his connections a few unpleasant moments.

Lord and Lady Howard de Walden were present to see Kris do his final work before Ascot. The horse was particularly well, but objected to waiting at the bottom of Warren Hill before going on the gallop. From his owner's vantage-point, half-way up the hill, Kris was seen to be reversing smartly down the Moulton Road towards the middle of Newmarket! It was some little time before his rider got him on to the grass. But as so often happened after these displays of what I will charitably call character, he proceeded to work brilliantly.

At Ascot Kris again met Young Generation, who since the Guineas had won both the Lockinge and the Prix Jean Prat. He beat him more easily than he had done at Newbury, taking the lead as they straightened for home and holding his rival's late challenge with some comfort. At Goodwood he was even more impressive in the Sussex Stakes, slamming Swiss Maid by five lengths. A less spectacular victory followed in the Waterford Crystal Mile, which was run at Ascot due to renovations at Goodwood, as Joe gave the horse more to do at disadvantageous weights against older horses. Then it was back to Ascot for a runaway victory in the Queen Elizabeth II Stakes.

The decision was then taken by his sporting owner to keep Kris in training as a four-year-old. I decided that an attempt at ten furlongs would be better delayed until the following season, rather than to face him with a new trip in the Champion Stakes. His final race as a three-year-old was thus the Challenge Stakes over seven furlongs at Newmarket. Despite his long, hard season, Kris looked wonderfully well and stronger than ever. He had no trouble in disposing of a useful field, and in the process broke a course record which had stood for forty-one years.

The intention to establish Kris as a ten-furlong horse in his third season was thwarted by injury, and he finished his career without attempting a distance beyond a mile. His four-year-old career started auspiciously enough. The Cold Shield Window Trophy at Haydock was run at a strong pace throughout, and despite my fear that he might just have been in need of the race he prevailed by a length, and despite jumping the shadow of the winning-post, and finishing in mid-air, he broke the course record. Kris's next race, the Lockinge, was a real rough-house. With some difficulty Joe restrained him for six furlongs, and when a gap appeared asked him to go. The horses on either side of him closed in and leaned on him, almost taking Kris off his feet for several strides. With great courage he continued his run, despite several more bumps, and held off his old rival Foveros, breaking the course record yet again, for the third time in successive races. There was a lengthy stewards' inquiry before he was announced the winner, but even then there had been more drama. During his return to the winner's enclosure he was given a hefty kick on the knee by another runner.

Kris's problems were just beginning. After the Lockinge he pulled a muscle in his back when cast in his box, and he was never the same horse again. Several recurrences of the problem forced him to miss important engagements throughout the summer, and the Queen Anne Stakes, the Eclipse, the Sussex Stakes and the Waterford Crystal Mile all passed with Kris confined to his box. His reappearance was delayed until mid-September, when in the Crown of Crown Stakes at Goodwood he trotted up by twelve lengths. The significance of that race had its origin in the attitude of the starter. I must admit that Kris was never easy to get behind the stalls, or into them. On this occasion he was particularly difficult, yet in asking him to take a stalls test at that stage of his career, with two races at the most before his retirement, the starter cannot seriously have been expecting any improvement in his behaviour. Nevertheless, a stalls test (which would largely contribute to Kris's final defeat) *was* required, and after a journey to Yarmouth in company with a stable companion duly passed in circumstances akin to a farce.

At this stage Kris had won fourteen of his fifteen starts, and had remained undefeated in nine races spanning sixteen months. The last race for this great horse came ten days after his stalls test. Meeting the best three-year-old milers in the Queen Elizabeth Stakes at Ascot, he was taken down to the start early. The haunting picture of him standing behind the stalls, becoming steadily black with sweat, and Joe borrowing a handkerchief from a stalls handler to wipe his sweat-soaked reins, often flashes through my mind. Kris was first to be put into the stalls, and he became increasingly disturbed. He gave his all in a race run at a blistering pace, and after a great duel with the 2,000 Guineas winner Known Fact in the last two furlongs he was beaten by a neck in what was described as the most exciting race of all season. Lord Howard's only comment was: 'That's what racing is all about. He was beaten by a very good horse.'

The decision to retire Kris was made in the enclosure at Ascot. He left Warren Place with the status of one of the best milers of the post-war era. He never gave less than his best, and was a much-loved character. He stands at the Thornton Stud in Yorkshire.

**Light Cavalry and Fairy Footsteps**

It is hardly surprising that Glass Slipper became broodmare of the year, as she had produced a colt and a filly to win two classics in the space of six months. Light Cavalry won the St Leger in 1980, and Fairy Footsteps was successful in the 1,000 Guineas in 1981.

Light Cavalry – so far probably the best son of Brigadier

Gerard – was a big bay colt with a white blaze. He was Julie's favourite, and she rode him in a great deal of his work as well as all his everyday exercise. I do not know why, but seldom does Julie take over a horse as a regular ride without it turning out other than very useful. She rode Busted – who was voted Horse of the Year in England in 1967 after winning the Coronation Stakes at Sandown, the Eclipse and the King George for her father – while among her other rides have been Irvine, Welsh Chanter, Twilight Alley and Aliante, to mention but a few. I probably take her slightly for granted, but Julie is a rider of the highest calibre, educating the horses and keeping them up to their work.

Light Cavalry – or Francis, as he was known in the yard – took some time to come to himself, but he was to win many races, among them the King Edward at Royal Ascot en route to the St Leger. I was exuding confidence on St Leger day. Light Cavalry had worked very well, and had never been better in himself in the whole of his career. It was a thoroughly relaxed drive to Doncaster, and I was really looking forward to the event. Twice in years gone by I felt we should have won the final classic, with Falkland and Le Moss, and this time I was quite confident. We had lunch in Mr Joel's box, and I could really enjoy some beautifully pink cold grouse and a lobster. The grouse had been put aside and hidden by his butler until my arrival; as Colonel Scrope was a regular diner at that meeting, and would go through the whole lot given a chance. We decided that if Light Cavalry won we would all congregate for tea in the box, otherwise we would creep away home with our tails between our legs. On leaving the box I told the butler and the waitress, 'I will see you later.'

Light Cavalry made practically all the running, and won very easily by four lengths from the favourite, Water Mill. He was in top form that day, and running over what was probably his best trip. He could have been a Cup horse of the future. But again, to increase his distance would only mean decreasing his value, as had happened with Buckskin. Mr Joel was overcome with excitement, and there were tears in his eyes as he received the trophy, a Wedgwood dinner service which was a replica of the one made for the Kaiser on a State visit. At tea he said he would like me to have it, but it was too embarrassing, and I politely refused, saying that he should keep it as a memento of a great day. I regret declining the offer. It was such a lovely collection, and it reposed in a cupboard under the stairs at his house in Newmarket after he sold his large house, as he had no room for it in his house on his Childwick Bury Stud.

As a four-year-old Light Cavalry won the Princess of Wales's Stakes in a slowly run race. It was a particularly game performance, and he just got up in a photo to gain a neck verdict over Castle Keep, to whom he was conceding 12lb. General opinion had it that Lester Piggott had ridden a fantastic race, but to be honest I thought that if he had dictated the pace and made it a relentless gallop the horse would have won far more easily, without vigorous use of the whip. Light Cavalry then developed tendon trouble, and although he ran in the King George he was beginning to feel his legs, and finished last of seven to Shergar. He was sold to America, where he now stands as a stallion. I hope he gets the support he deserves, although many people in racing feel he did not possess the real speed of a mile-and-a-half horse.

Fairy Footsteps was a thick-set, well-made bay filly with practically the same colouring as her half-brother. She never had the great temperament that Light Cavalry displayed, and one could never say she was quite such a lovable character. But she possessed great ability, and we were all very fond of her. She ran at Sandown first time out as a two-year-old, and having been left made up a great deal of ground in the straight under Joe Mercer, so that shė was able to challenge the leader. Those efforts took their toll, and she weakened in the last fifty yards, just missing a place. We were all thrilled by her running, and it was clear to us then that she was a filly with a very bright future.

She next ran in a fillies' race at Newmarket, where she was beaten because she managed to get into such a hopeless position that when an opening came she had too much ground to make up. In the circumstances she did well to finish second. Bruce Raymond rode her, but I probably had a certain amount to do with her defeat. She had run a little freely on her debut, and I wanted to have her settled in behind in the early stages at Newmarket. It was the formative part of her career, and she had to learn to relax and use her speed at the right time in her races, but in trying to cover her up Raymond got himself into that inextricable position.

She won the Waterford Candelabra at Goodwood next time out very easily in the hands of Pat Eddery. Despite crawling out of the stalls, she was soon left out in front, but she relaxed and did it well. Convinced that she was a Guineas filly, I decided the sooner she was put away for the winter the better. She wintered nicely, and reappeared with a smooth success in the Nell Gwyn Stakes at Newmarket. Fairy Footsteps was then installed as favourite for the 1,000 Guineas, but I was unhappy about her prospects because Lester had had a terrible accident in the stalls at Epsom the previous week, necessitating many stitches in his ear. He had also pulled the muscles in his back, having been dragged under the stalls by Winsor Boy, the berserk animal he had unfortunately been engaged to ride. Lester recovered in time to ride her in the 1,000 Guineas, his ear protected by a suede cover. You could never describe Lester's complexion as ruddy, but that day he looked like a ghost!

Fairy Footsteps, ridden to perfection by a true artist, made all the running to win by a hard-pressed neck from Tolmi. I was filled with admiration for the man. Very few people could have got back into the saddle, never mind ride a classic winner, after that terrifying accident at Epsom only a week before. On his resumption at Ascot the day before the Guineas meeting he was weak, and never gave his horse any sort of ride at all, tiring long before his mount. On the face of it he could never ride the 1,000 Guineas winner, but I was not going to take him off. Lester is a professional, and if he had thought he could not do the filly justice I know he would have stood down. After the race they came slowly and relaxed into the winner's enclosure to a deserved and tumultuous welcome. Was the relief the source of the tears in Lester's eyes? I think it was a combination of that, tiredness and the excitement of doing what many thought was the impossible.

The Guineas was always going to be the race for Fairy Footsteps, and although she was favourite for the Oaks, after she finished third in heavy ground in the Musidora Stakes, Mr Joel and I decided to retire her. She was already a classic winner, and surely had done enough.

**Ardross**

A gale-force wind was strewing litter about the roadside like confetti on the damp January day in 1981 that Charles St George and I were driven from Dublin Airport to The Curragh. The sweep of the windscreen wipers drew me into a trance in which I contemplated how overstretched the Government budget must be to allow the highways to become so cluttered with debris. I was snapped out of my thoughts by the sight of a fleet of Black Marias, with army and police escorts, carrying IRA prisoners in the opposite direction. A helicopter hovered over the convoy, and as I supposed that they must be on their way to the courts in

Dublin I was suddenly overcome by a feeling of uneasiness. We had been met by that great trainer Micky Rogers, who was then retired, and it made me feel even less comfortable when his petrol gauge touched 'empty', so that he was forced to join a long queue at a garage in the middle of nowhere. Only one gallon was being allocated to each car because of a tanker-drivers' strike, and that on condition that the driver was a regular client. Micky had to do a lot of talking to convince the proprietor that he never used any other garage than his, although it was plain to me that he had never been there before in his life.

The purpose of this depressing journey was to look at Ardross, a five-year-old, who had run Le Moss to three parts of a length in the Ascot Gold Cup the previous year. Le Moss had retired to stud, and we were looking for a replacement for him as a representative of the stable in the top-class long-distance races. Following the death of Paddy Prendergast – who had trained Ardross throughout most of his career – his stable had been taken over by his son Kevin. Although obviously sad at the prospect of losing Ardross, who could well have given him a wonderful season by winning the Gold Cup, Kevin was willing to sell the horse if the price was right.

Micky Rogers had trained Hard Ridden and Santa Claus to win the Derby, and now ran a few broodmares in his paddocks while advising Charles St George on his bloodstock. I think that his highly strung temperament put so much pressure on him that his health began to be affected, and that he was therefore wise to retire from training.

Three boxes down from the entrance to the yard stood Ardross, a big bay horse, with a lovely head, full of quality. I was slightly surprised to see how little flesh he carried, but he looked healthy enough, and very well in his coat. We asked to see him out of his box, and the way he walked convinced me that we must have him. The deal was done in the tack-room, and subject to his passing an examination by a veterinary surgeon he would come to Warren Place. He was to become not only champion stayer but practically the best middle-distance horse in the country, and in achieving so much provided us with a great deal of fun and pleasure.

On his arrival in our stable we decided to let him down until bringing him into serious training in the spring. This would give him time to thicken out and put on weight, so that he would be more likely to retain his form until the end of the season. He was basically a stayer, and I had no intention of subjecting him to too much racing over a mile and a half, as that could have soured him, but I would have liked him to have won one or two races over that distance to enhance his value as a potential stallion. As I have said before, breeders are somewhat reluctant to send mares to specialist stayers.

Ardross came along well in his work, and when we ran him for the first time he took the Yorkshire Cup in his stride. While Donegal Prince set a strong pace, Ardross moved easily at the back of the field. Two furlongs into the straight he made up a tremendous amount of ground, and as they approached the two-furlong marker was poised about four lengths behind the leaders. Producing a splendid turn of finishing speed when making his challenge a furlong out, he swamped his rivals in a few strides to win by three lengths from the favourite, Nicholas Bill, despite Piggott not even having slapped him down the neck.

His next outing was in the Gold Cup, which he won without hardly having had a race. Piggott was at his cheekiest, pouncing in the final furlong in that familiar pose, head turned towards the rider of the challenger, and the corners of his mouth turned up in a grin. With the others under the strongest pressure while Ardross was cantering, it must have been infuriating for Willie Carson on Shoot a Line to be toyed with like that.

Ardross won eleven group races and more than £350,000 in prize-money for me to add to the two pattern races worth about £50,000, in which he had been successful while with Kevin Prendergast. The most important of the races that he won while at Warren Place were two Ascot Gold Cups, the Prix Royal Oak (the French St Leger), in which he beat Gold River, winner of the Prix de l'Arc de Triomphe three weeks earlier, the Geoffrey Freer Stakes at Newbury twice and the Jockey Club Stakes, in which he beat Glint of Gold.

Ardross put up what was possibly his greatest performance in his second bid for the Prix de l'Arc de Triomphe. He was so close to winning the greatest race in the world that it was heart-breaking. At six years of age he was better than ever, and it seemed that he was only beaten as a result of Harbour losing ground very rapidly. She did not really interfere with him, but as she dropped away she took him back a couple of lengths with her, forcing him to come round her. I do not like making excuses, but had he been able to use his long, raking stride in a clear run up the straight it might well have enabled him to win instead of being beaten a head by Akiyda.

Ardross was a great horse. There was only one thought in his mind during a race, and that was to finish in front. His courage was remarkable; he kept on improving with age, and it was only two months before he would turn seven years of age that we decided that he had done enough. He must be rated as one of the outstanding stayers to have run since the war, with only Buckskin, Twilight Alley, Le Moss and Sagaro in the same league.

When he left us there was a feeling of great loss at Warren Place. His gentle temperament in the yard had always been on a par with the courage he had displayed on the racecourse.

He is now standing at the Beech House Stud under the management of Franca Vittadini. She is a top-class jockey, who rides out for us every morning, and a great friend of Julie and me.

**Simply Great**

But for an injury sustained in training it is more than possible that Simply Great would have become the fourth Derby winner to be trained at Warren Place.

A bay colt by Mill Reef out of a German mare, he makes up for his lack of size by his great quality. He was bred in France, and right from the time he was a yearling he has shown a tremendous amount of promise. Having pulled a muscle in the summer, he made a belated racecourse debut in October 1981, when he won by a convincing three lengths in a field of twenty-two over seven furlongs at Newmarket. The runner-up was Luca Cumani's Century City, who was to be successful in the Cambridgeshire under a record weight for a three-year-old twelve months later.

In none of the work that Simply Great did immediately after winning that race did he show the sparkle that he had done earlier in the year. On the day of the Dewhurst Stakes he looked very dull, having gone in his coat literally overnight, and I very nearly withdrew him. After he had run no sort of race I was bitterly regretting I had not done so.

Simply Great wintered well and reappeared in the Craven Stakes at Newmarket in early April 1982. He ran a beautiful race to be fourth to Silver Hawk, but was evidently in need of the outing as he had little in reserve when Piggott produced him to deliver his challenge.

His owner, Mr Wildenstein, was a little disappointed by the colt's showing in the Craven Stakes, but I asked him to reserve judgment until after the Dante Stakes at York the following month. In the Dante Stakes Simply Great put up a fine performance by beating Palace Gold by two and a half lengths, and became favourite for the Derby.

His work after the Dante was quite brilliant. If anything he was inclined to go too well, as I would have liked to see him off the bit in the early stages.

Eight days before the Derby there occurred one of those accidents dreaded by the trainers of big-race favourites. As he was breaking into a canter Simply Great stumbled, and having lost control of his hind-legs, cut deep into the heel of his near fore-leg as they slid under him. At first we could not understand why he was so sore and lame for so long after a comparatively minor setback. Eventually Dr Reed flew over from America. He decided to X-ray the whole of the near fore-leg, and found a slight crack in the cannon bone, caused by the weight of the blow from the hind-foot. In consequence there could be no question of his running in the Derby.

I have always felt that there was a very good chance that Simply Great would have beaten Golden Fleece at Epsom. Had he not done so he would certainly have been second.

Although he was subsequently sound again, Simply Great did not have another race as a three-year-old, as there was insufficient time in which to prepare him for an autumn engagement. As I have always been of the opinion that he could be a top-class horse if he learns to relax in the early stages of his races, he was kept in training as a four-year-old in 1983.

There were flowers on the Poor Boy's Grave again this year, and I dared to hope it was an omen that one of our Derby colts was going to compensate Warren Place for the misfortune that befell Simply Great. Many years ago, when sheep grazed the Heath, a little gipsy lost most of the flock in his care, and rather than face the anger of his master hanged himself. They buried him where the road to Bury St Edmunds crossed the one from Moulton to the Thetford Road at the top of the Limekilns, and legend has it that whenever there are flowers on the Poor Boy's

Grave in the spring a Newmarket horse will win the Derby. It was borne out in the shape of Teenoso, trained by Geoffrey Wragg, who has recently taken over the reins from his father Harry.

**Diesis and Dunbeath**

In 1982 we were lucky enough to have a handful of really good two-year-olds, including Diesis, Dunbeath, The Fort and Salieri, at Warren Place. Between them they won the Solario Stakes, the Mill Reef Stakes, the Royal Lodge Stakes, the Dewhurst Stakes and the William Hill Futurity. The only other important autumn race for first season colts is Newbury's Horris Hill Stakes, which was to have been the objective of Salieri. Unfortunately, though, it was abandoned due to heavy rain.

Lord Howard de Walden's Diesis, a full brother to the great Kris, was placed top of the European Free Handicap. An undeveloped colt in many ways, he shaped up well after being slowly away through inexperience when making his racecourse debut at Newmarket in July and being fifth to Lofty. Next time out he made no mistake, and impressed enormously by making all the running to beat Swift To Conquer by seven lengths without being extended at the Newmarket meeting a month later.

On his third appearance Diesis took a step up in company by going for the £39,000 Middle Park Stakes over six furlongs at Newmarket in late September. Leading from start to finish again, Diesis beat Orixo by two and a half lengths.

Many people would have thought that a horse had done enough by winning one Group One race in his first season, but Lord Howard and I felt that he would be able to beat Gorytus in the seven-furlong Dewhurst Stakes, also at Newmarket, in the middle of October. On account of the ease with which he had won Doncaster's Champagne Stakes, Gorytus was being talked about as being the best horse since Mill Reef, and was already hot favourite for both the 2,000 Guineas and the Derby.

The widely anticipated duel between Diesis and Gorytus never materialized. Gorytus failed completely and inexplicably in the Dewhurst Stakes by dropping out after about four furlongs and finishing a remote last of four. For his part Diesis accelerated smoothly to come from last to first to beat Gordian by five lengths. Even had Gorytus run up to his form, I firmly believe that Diesis would still have won. Diesis, incidentally, was the first horse to bring off the double in the Middle Park and the Dewhurst since Lemburg in 1909. He has to be regarded as having been better than Kris was as a two-year-old, and was of a more placid temperament.

It is remarkable that Lord Howard's twelve-year-old mare Doubly Sure should have produced two such outstanding colts as Kris and Diesis to matings with Sharpen Up. Now she has a third chestnut colt by the same horse in Keen. She was going to be covered by Mill Reef in 1983, but after three such highly satisfactory matings had to be switched back to Sharpen Up.

A quarter-share in Diesis has been sold to Mrs Alice Chandler of The Mill Ridge Stud in the United States. Kris is already standing in England, and breeders will have no use for both brothers.

Dunbeath was gross and backward early on in his two-year-old days and we thought that a race might wake him up a bit. He made his debut at Newmarket in July week, and finished second to St Boniface, beaten three parts of a length, without having had a punishing race.

Soon afterwards this bay colt began to make up into an imposing individual of considerable potential. He won as he liked at Goodwood and York, and then beat Lyphard's Special by a length and a half on very soft ground in the Royal Lodge Stakes at Ascot. On his fifth and final appearance as a two-year-old Dunbeath gave fresh emphasis to his chance in the 1983 Derby by winning the Futurity from Cock Robin at Doncaster.

Tote Cherry-Downes and I bought Dunbeath from Lee Eaton for 100,000 dollars, a reasonable enough price by prevailing standards for a colt by Grey Dawn II out of an own sister to Bold Forbes, a winner of the Kentucky Derby. His breeder was very keen on him, and asked if he could retain a half-share should we buy him. To this we agreed, and so Lee Eaton came to own him in partnership with Michael Riordan.

As the two-year-old career of Dunbeath progressed, increasingly large offers were made for him. Eventually Michael and Lee received one that they could not refuse from Sheikh Mohammed, and he was sold on the condition that he remained at Warren Place, with his original owners having the option to buy back into him when he retires to stud.

**The Champions in 1983 and 1984 . . .**

When two year olds show the kind of form demonstrated by this quartet, one is inclined to spend the quieter moments of the winter months anticipating what delights are in store in their second seasons.

Unfortunately, they have a habit of turning out to be only pipe-dreams. The Fort, for instance, became disenchanted with racing and failed to train on.

Diesis was chosen to represent us in the 2,000 Guineas, but knocked himself on the eve of the race and we had a job to get him into the line-up. He never showed with a chance and finished eighth to Lomond. He now stands at the Mill Ridge Stud. I saw him there in the summer of 1984 and was really impressed with him. He has thickened out into a lovely horse and should do very well.

Dunbeath started his three year old career promisingly enough, running Shearwalk, who had the benefit of a previous win already, to a length in the Heathorn Stakes. He was third to Hot Touch in the Dante and, after finishing third to Horage in the St James's Palace, was sent to America to race. He is now standing at the Side Hill Stud in Newmarket. He should be well patronised, because not only was he an outstanding two year old, he is also a half brother to Saratago Six, the best two year old in America.

Salieri, who won the Diadem at Ascot and the Bisquit Cognac Challenge stakes (£21,320 to the winner) at Newmarket, was sold for a good sum to stand in Australia.

So was Keen, who broke the track record when winning over six furlongs at Ascot on his only start as a two year old. He, too, made a good start to his second season, winning the Easter Stakes at Kempton by four lengths. We were slightly disappointed at the time when he finished only fifth in the Guineas, but subsequent events showed it to be the best 2,000 for years, with the first four, El Gran Senor, Chief Singer, Lear Fan and Rainbow Quest, proving themselves to be out of the top drawer. Keen went on to be beaten a head in the Heron Stakes at Kempton, and it was certainly no disgrace to be second to Chief Singer in the St James's Palace.

If 1983 failed to fulfil all our expectations, it at least provided some very exciting moments. I had in my care the fastest two year old I have ever trained in Precocious, a Mummy's Pet colt bred at home by the Tavistocks out of Mrs Moss. We knew we had something special when he hacked up by three lengths from King Of Clubs on his debut at Newmarket. He never stopped improving, and by the time a knee injury curtailed his career in August he had gone through five races unbeaten.

The last of these was a fantastic performance in the

Gimcrack, when he made all and won by six lengths. He was back in training in March, 1984, but his preparation was made difficult by the prevailing very hard ground and the decision was taken to retire him. Precocious is a half brother to seven winners, including Clive Brittain's smart Jupiter Island, and we shall never know just how good he was. We never really got to the bottom of him. There is no doubting, however, that he was a brilliant two year old, and I would imagine that when he takes up stud duties in 1985 he will be a much sought after stallion.

Another who is bound to do well at stud is my old friend Simply Great who, unfortunately, never got over a succession of injury problems. His third to Bedtime in the September Stakes at Kempton in 1984 showed the ability was still there and he was to have one more race, in the Waldoe Stakes at Goodwood, before it was decided he should retire. His half brother, Sagace, won the 1984 Arc de Triomphe very easily and Sandy Island, whom I trained to win the Lancashire Oaks at Haydock, is closely related.He is going to stand in Ireland.

Trojan Fen, another of our two year olds in 1983, proved himself the best product of the ill-fated Derby winner Troy so far. He was Julie's baby from the start and, as is usually the case with the ones she adopts, he really flourished. He was completing a four timer when beating Head For Heights in the Washington Singer Stakes at Newbury, and though a shade disappointing when third to Gold And Ivory in the Royal Lodge at Ascot, he was probably over the top. Trojan Fen won the Gerry Feiden at Newbury and the Queen Anne at Royal Ascot in his second season, and when he retired after this second success he had the record of six wins fron eight starts. We won't count the ninth, for his saddle slipped and unseated his rider on leaving the stalls in the Lockinge at Newbury.

This good topped colt retired to Edmund Loder's Eyrefield Lodge Stud in Co Kildare with an admirable rating of 128.

Another highlight of 1983 was the Lowther Stakes win by Mr and Mrs Peter Player's Sharpen Up filly Prickle, who went on to be involved in a very tight finish behind Desirable in the Cheveley Park. she was only a short head behind the runner-up, Pebbles, who, of course, went on to win the 1984 1,000 Guineas. Prickle unfortunately failed to train on and now stands at her owners' Whatton Stud.

In these days of inflated prices in the bloodstock world, I would like to make a favourable mention of a horse who could prove to be one of the all time value for money stallions.

Adonijah, who came to us having had one backend run for Bruce Hobbs as a two year old, caught the imagination when running away with his maiden at Newbury early in 1983 and went on to make a procession of the three runner High Line Stakes, a race named after his sire, at York. He won four times in all, revelling in the soft ground he was to get so rarely a year later. When he did, he was lethal. In the space of nine days he won the Brigadier Gerard Stakes at Sandown by no less than eight lengths, and he hacked up by three lengths in the Pacemaker Siomed Stakes at Epsom. The ground was good to firm when we took him to Longchamps for the Group One Prix d'Ispahan, and although the underfoot conditions did not suit him he ran a gallant race to be third to Crystal Glitters. He is a half brother to the promising sire Absalom and should do well at Nicky Phillips' Someries Stud at Newmarket.

Mention of Absalom brings me back to William Jarvis, who was active in the yearling market at the end of 1984 and will start training on his own account in 1985 at

Phantom House with between 30 and 40 horses. Some of my owners, including Sheik Mohammed, Lord Howard, Mr Joel, the Tavistocks, Peter Harris and Peter Player, have been generous in supporting Willie's new venture, and he enters this very competitive field with my warmest hopes for a bright future. He will be based just one and a half miles from me, so I can certainly keep an eye on him! Let us hope that Willie's progress is not so rapid, though, that he takes from me the trainers' championship that I won for the fifth time in 1984!

It was a blessed relief when Lanfranco won the Futurity at Doncaster to secure the title. I was being hard pressed by both John Dunlop and Guy Harwood at the time, and my emotional reaction to his victory in the winner's enclosure was due, I suppose, to all the pressure being lifted in the space of a few seconds. Winning the title means a lot to me, and had Lanfranco been beaten I would have had to reorganise all my runners for the rest of the season in an attempt to get there.

It was a fine performance by Lanfranco, whom Charles St George had picked out at the sales and acquired for the bargain sum of 17,500 guineas. The Futurity was only the fourth race of his life, and this handsome chestnut son of 1963 Derby winner Relko went into winter quarters as a leading fancy for the 1985 premier classic.

The winter favourite for the 1,000 Guineas was also housed at Warren Place in the shape of Oh So Sharp, who was unbeaten in three races. We started her off in a small race at Nottingham, where she won impressively, and she was then pitched in at the deep end against the colts in the Solario Stakes at Sandown. She won in pleasing style, beating Young Runaway two lengths, and then showed her class when winning the Hoover Fillies Mile at Ascot from Dick Hern's Helen Street, who had lowered the course record at Deauville on her previous start. It would be a delight for me if she won the Guineas, for she is from the first crop of Kris and is a half sister to Roussalka.

**. . . and a Champion hope for 1985**

As the 1984 season drew to a close, my elation at having secured the championship was tinged with regret at a parting of the ways with Lester Piggott. There had been a misunderstanding over the riding arrangements for Daniel Wildenstein's mare All Along in the 1983 Arc de Triomphe, with the owner convinced Lester would ride her when, in fact, he chose to partner John Dunlop's Awaasif. Mr Wildenstein stated that Lester would never ride for him again and, feeling the owner was in the right, I had to support him. He no longer wanted Lester and I could not have my stable divided. It became impossible, therefore, for Lester to continue riding for my stable and we had to call it a day, which was very sad, but inevitable.

I had always hoped that when Lester retired, Steve Cauthen would join us, and that process was expedited by these events. Steve has adjusted well to English racing and must be the best of the younger jockeys. We get on well together, and I hope it will be a happy and lucrative partnership.

I have been delighted with the progress made by Paul Eddery, who joined us as number two jockey in 1984. Paul, younger brother of the highly successful jockey Pat, came to me having achieved a best score of 23 while claiming in the north, and was only just short of 50 winners without a claim in his first season here. He has quite an exciting future ahead of him.

# 7
## *Princes and Paupers*

Whoever said that all men are equal on the turf and under had only a nodding acquaintance with racehorse-owners. Far from having found all owners equal, I have discovered that possession of a horse is well calculated to bring out absolutely anything from the very best to the very worst in human nature.

Some owners enjoy any success that may come their way to the full, take the inevitable disappointments in their stride and settle their bills every month. At the other end of the spectrum are those owners who can never be relied upon to pay their bills, complain vociferously if horses do not behave like machines by running up to form in every race, and then proceed to tell their trainer how to do his job with a great deal more confidence than they would their dentist.

Most of my owners have been wonderful, and given me good cause to be deeply appreciative of their patience and understanding. Others have found themselves unable to continue to meet the cost of keeping a horse in training, and though they have ceased to be my owners they have remained friends. Then again there are owners who have been a long way from straightforward when complications have arisen, and I have been left indifferent as to whether I ever saw them again.

I have always taken the view that if we work hard, and are successful, owners will want to have horses with us. These people are worth having. They are not asked to have a horse in the stable while cornered in a smoky bar, or propositioned after a bottle of port at dinner.

Some people are very professional at obtaining owners.

A number of bloodstock agents have also at times been none too scrupulous as to how they acquired business, and never been slow to claim contacts or knowledge that they do not possess. I know a true story about one of them that made me laugh a lot, and I must include it here. A certain Irish bloodstock agent, who used to be a Rolls-Royce salesman, was chatting up a couple of clients without making much impression on them over drinks in the Casino during the Deauville sales. As he was beginning to get worried about the way things were going, he noticed Sir Charles Clore sitting in a corner by himself, scribbling on a piece of paper. That gave him an idea, so he said to the two men he wanted for clients, 'Will you excuse me a minute; I have got to go to see somebody?' and slipped round the other side of the bar to approach Sir Charles Clore. He said to Sir Charles, 'I am terribly sorry to interrupt, as you do not know me, but I know who you are, and I have always been a great admirer of yours because you are a self-made man and terribly successful. I am just starting up in business, and want to be the same. Do you think you could do me a favour?'

Sir Charles – who was not the easiest of people, and took a little bit of getting to know – said, 'It depends what it is.'

'Do you not agree,' asked the bloodstock agent, 'that to get on in life it helps to have good connections, and to know the right sort of people?'

'Yes, I suppose that's true,' replied Sir Charles.

'Well, don't think me impertinent,' said the bloodstock agent, 'but you see those two people over there? I am trying to get them to buy a yearling at the sales tomorrow, and it is being a bit difficult. Do you think that when you leave the bar you could pass us, tap me on the shoulder and say "Hello, nice to see you; how are you?" That will impress them, and they might buy the yearling.'

A short while afterwards Sir Charles left the bar, and,

patting the bloodstock agent on the shoulder, said, 'Hello, nice to see you, how are you?'

'Bugger off, Charlie,' said the man. 'Çan't you see I'm busy?'

Although never reduced to employing that sort of strategy to establish myself, I was happy to take a horse from anyone when I started training. As the stable has become more successful we have been able to concentrate on the sort of owner who makes life easier for us, to the exclusion of individuals who are constantly making unrealistic demands. Training horses is hard enough, but if you have to train the owners as well life can be terribly exhausting.

Unfortunately, there are very few owner-breeders, like the Lords Derby, Rosebery and Astor of pre-war days, still involved in racing, as they are a dying breed. Most members of the peerage seem to have much of their resources committed to the maintenance of family homes, and insufficient surplus income for racing after decades of heavy taxation and intermittent death duties. Similarly, smaller landowners, whose forebears bred any number of good horses down the years, are as often as not reduced to keeping just one or two mares because of high stallion fees and other escalating costs. Men and women in these categories, whose families have raced for generations, invariably understand animals. It is a lot easier, and more fun, to train for them (because we look at the job in hand from the same viewpoint) than it is for people who regard a horse as no more than a realizable commercial asset or a status symbol.

Some owners of the modern school have sufficient assets to be able to keep large strings of horses in training, without hardly knowing which end bites and which end kicks. They are not what the French call 'sympathique'. There is no rapport between man and beast. They do not understand horses, and never will.

Owners have changed a great deal as a result of racing having become increasingly international, and fortunately for the future, there are people who have come into racing during recent years who do understand it, and as such are an invaluable asset. I admire them very much, and am grateful that they more than compensate for those owners who regard racing as an entry into what they imagine to be high society, and do not care if animals are abused because of their impatience to realize their ambitions.

In the last few years racing, like everything else, has been hit by the recession, and the British bloodstock industry has been fortunate to enjoy the enthusiastic support of Arab owners. Because of the recession much of our bloodstock was sent to the United States, but these owners from the Middle East, inspired by their love of the great variety of British racing, have sent their representatives to America to buy back colts and fillies from the best bloodlines in order to be able to retire them eventually to the studs they are founding in this country.

Most of these men were brought up on horseback, and are *sympathique* in abundance. They are generally patient, with sport, not profit, their main concern. The thrill of the race is more important than the prize-money and the trophies. Consequently, they are to be welcomed as the successors of the owners of the old school, such as the late Lord Rosebery, on whose death in 1974 the celebrated Mentmore Stud had to be broken up and sold.

Among my favourite owners is Mr Joel, one of the last representatives of all that is best in the old tradition of the owner-breeder. Known to all his friends as Jim (although the name on his birth certificate is Harry), he is a charming gentleman in his eighties. For many years he had horses with Sir Noel, who trained Royal Palace to win both the Derby and the 2,000 Guineas for him in 1967.

Mr Joel is a member of a family who have bred and raced horses since before the beginning of the present century. He has about twenty mares at the Childwick Bury Stud, near St Albans, which he inherited together with £5,000,000 from his father, Jack Joel, in 1940. Jack Joel, whose fortune came from the South African diamond-mines, purchased Childwick Bury from the executors of Sir Blundell Maple in 1907, and it was there that he bred the Derby winners Sunstar (1911) and Humorist (1921).

At the time when Mr Joel came into possession of Childwick Bury the stud had been going through a lean period, but he laid the foundations of his success as a breeder by carrying out extensive renovations at very considerable expense, while persevering with the same bloodlines that his father had done. The best of the horses that we have trained for Mr Joel are the classic winners Light Cavalry and Fairy Footsteps and Main Reef, a high-class horse now standing at stud in Ireland. The seventh dam of Light Cavalry and Fairy Footsteps, counting back from daughter to mother, is Absurdity, whose grandson Humorist won the Derby for Mr Joel's father more than sixty years ago.

We are in the fortunate position of being able to have the pick of Mr Joel's yearlings to take into training. Most of his horses need time in which to find their form, but he breeds on such sound lines that he provides a constant source of winners.

It would be quite easy to miss Mr Joel, a bachelor, on the racecourse. He is very small, and usually wears a heavy overcoat with a brown trilby hat pulled right down in front. He rushes around the stands and paddock in as sprightly a fashion as a man in his twenties, and even if it is not his famous black jacket and scarlet cap that has been carried successfully he will make his way to the unsaddling enclosure to congratulate the connections of the winner.

He has a wonderful mind, a great sense of humour and a refreshingly youthful outlook on life. To sit and chat with him is like being in company with a member of one's own generation.

He has a house in Newmarket, Sefton Lodge on the Bury Road, for race weeks, during which we are always invited to dine with him. Although he eats hardly anything himself, he loves seeing other people enjoying his hospitality. As eating good food is one of my greatest pleasures in life, I always enjoy dining with him – so much so that he refers to me as his champion trencherman. All the same, one can be overcome by the richness and the abundance of his food. Once when we were at Sefton Lodge I was delighted to see a beautiful mass of orchids laid down along the centre of the table. Not only were the blooms lovely to look at, but they prevented our host from seeing how little even I partook of each dish. A typical menu begins with caviar and smoked salmon, followed by home-made soup, fillets of sole or lobster thermidor, then a good steak or (depending on the time of year) grouse or partridge. On the evening that the orchids concealed my epicurean diffidence from my host I remember that we had *petit poussin*, and then home-made ice-cream, savoury and fruit. Despite the excellent preparation of the earlier, elaborate dishes, I enjoyed the peaches and muscat grapes more than anything, and more than compensated for my previous abstinence.

'Right, let's go into the next room to discuss Tattersall's latest catalogue,' said our host after the coffee. On rising from the table my untoward indulgence in the fresh fruit took its toll, and I was suddenly afflicted with so severe a pain that I could not move for a moment. As I staggered through the door I must have given a pretty fair impression of Groucho Marx, and I had to ask Mr Joel for a half-hour's adjournment of the business of the evening while I recovered my composure.

Another of my favourite owners is Lord Howard de Walden, who became Senior Steward of the Jockey Club for the third time in 1976. He is the model patron for any stable, as he never interferes, and inspires confidence by letting you get on with the job, knowing that you are not going to be criticized for doing things your own way. We have derived an enormous amount of pleasure from training for him over the past dozen or so years. He has a fabulous sense of humour that enables him to see the funny side of any situation. He calls me his Gucci trainer because of my partiality for shoes of that make, and one July week Julie and I were somewhat amused when he appeared on the course wearing a canvas imitation pair.

Lord Howard has extensive property interests in the West End of London, and is the ninth holder of the barony. His father, a noted connoisseur of the arts who died in 1946, was also a well-known owner, his most famous horse being Zinfandel, winner of the Ascot Gold Cup in 1905.

As well as the Plantation Stud here at Newmarket, the present Lord Howard de Walden has the Kintbury Stud adjoining his Berkshire home, Avington Manor, and the Thornton Stud in Yorkshire, with Leslie Harrison his principal manager. His all-apricot colours (which he inherited from his father) enjoy a popular following on the courses. The best horses that we have trained to carry them are Kris, Diesis, Falkland, Strigida and Catalpa, who won the Ribblesdale Stakes at Royal Ascot in 1976.

Another lovely set of silks of a single colour hanging in my saddle-room are the rose-pink jacket and cap of Lady Mairi Bury, for whose grandfather Lord Chaplin they were carried by Hermit to win the Derby in 1867. They are not, unfortunately, seen on the racecourse these days, as Lady Mairi no longer has horses in training.

If only all owners had the attitudes, even if not necessarily the resources, of Mr Joel and Lord Howard, one would have no need for the misgivings expressed earlier in the chapter. Despite the pain caused by reopening old wounds, I will give two instances of relationships with owners that were a lot less than happy.

A certain gentleman in the rag trade bought a horse for about £1,000, and we were delighted when we discovered it had some ability. It won six races, and by the time we sold it for more than £6,000 the owner had shown a handsome profit. Nevertheless, he went around the racecourse muttering that he had had a raw deal over the horse.

Actually I thought we were left with greater grounds for regret, as dealing with him had been problematical. I used to give Julie a tenner to go racing with him, to buy myself out of the ordeal, though she found it a ticklish business. He had a heavy beard, and whenever the horse won he insisted upon kissing her. This man really took the biscuit while I was in hospital, having an ulcer removed, and Julie phoned him with the news that his horse had been given a walkover on a fashionable south-country course.

'Walkover,' mused the puzzled owner. 'Is that a good thing?'

Another man had had his horse in a rival stable before sending it to us. We got it over its many problems, and then placed it to win some nice races. After the first of these successes the owner came into the yard and gave the head lad the princely sum of £3.

When the horse was capitalized for retirement to stud I wrote to the owner to ask if there was any possibility of my having a share. His answer was to send a horsebox to remove his remaining horses from the yard. I was dumbfounded. Had he said he was unable to let me have a share I would have quite understood.

The £3 present to the head lad just mentioned was a fortune compared to the 10p that once changed hands in my yard. That was the amount of a certain owner's reward to a lad who did the horse who had just won a big race for him.

'Buy yourself a drink,' said the owner. Fortunately, the lad did not have too big a hangover to be able to come to work the next morning.

Reverting to the subject of better men, Julie and I were very sad when Sir Reginald Macdonald-Buchanan died in 1981, and will always remember him as one of the best owners we ever had. Long before he had horses with us he owned one of the brilliant sprinters of all time in the grey Abernant, whom Sir Noel trained to win fourteen races and run Nimbus to a short head in the 2,000 Guineas of 1949.

Sir Reginald, a small, dapper man, was always immaculately turned out, with silk handkerchief flowing from his breast-pocket, shoes you could see your face in, and waxed moustache. In keeping with his perfect grooming, he had the most beautiful manners of anyone I have ever known. He used to love to come up to Warren Place for a large whisky after racing, while Lady Macdonald-Buchanan had a cup of tea or looked round the horses.

Cottesbrooke Hall, his lovely country house near Northampton, was surrounded by an estate of considerable acreage. Shooting has always been one of the greatest passions of my life, and it was a great pleasure to be asked to shoot there.

Always as punctilious as he was courteous, Sir Reginald liked to see the observance of the old-fashioned formalities that he had known since his Edwardian boyhood. One evening after sixteen of us had sat down to dinner at Cottesbrooke we went into the drawing-room, where there were three sofas and a number of chairs. Being unable to find anywhere to sit I lay on the floor, as I would at home, to talk to somebody. Immediately I heard a voice say, 'Terrible manners the young have nowadays.' Shrinking with embarrassment, I retired to a far corner of the room and spent the rest of the evening in silent meditation.

Sir Reginald hated draughts. On our arrival on one occasion the butler was half-way through the front door loaded down with our luggage when Sir Reginald appeared upon the stairs and admonished, 'I have told you to keep the front door shut.'

Placed in a predicament as to where his duty lay, it seemed an eternity before the butler decided whether to carry on into the hall to deposit our cases or to drop them immediately to close the front door.

Julie and I were always happy staying at Cottesbrooke, where everyone had great fun. Sir Reginald was never allowed to forget the day he changed the duck drive round so that there was no danger of the dogs drowning after plunging through a covering of ice. Unfortunately, he forgot to change the direction of the guns, so that all they saw were thousands of ducks flying away into the distance, instead of flying towards them. On another occasion the party was less seriously inconvenienced at a shooting lunch. Suddenly Sir Reginald's son-in-law Christo Phillipson shouted, 'Edward has done it again!' as he noticed the elderly butler serving the treacle pudding with the Brussels sprouts instead of the steak and kidney pie.

It was not only the success of his horses that made Sir Reginald a memorable man.

Probably my luckiest owner is Carlo d'Alessio, the Italian lawyer. It is not only because he owned Bolkonski and Wollow, winners of the 2,000 Guineas in successive years, and Le Moss, the first horse to win the Ascot, Goodwood and Doncaster Cups twice, that we have never been heard to have a row. He cannot speak English, and I do not know a word of Italian.

Lloyds' underwriter Charles St George has had horses with me almost since I started training, and we have become great friends. Although he can become nervous before a big race, and indecisive as to whether to run, he is invariably a good loser and an equally good winner, having no complaints in defeat and being modest in victory. Ardross carried his colours to win a number of

Group races, and afforded him much pleasure. I like to think we will find him a replacement for Ardross one day, but it will not be easy.

While at Lexington sales a little while ago I came across a man who had had a share in Ardross on his hands and knees in the elevator. Feeling slightly concerned, I inquired if he were feeling all right.

'I'm okay,' he replied. 'A dime found is a dime earned is what I always say.'

No wonder he is a millionaire.

Another owner whom I liked was Herbert Barker, a builder from Lincolnshire. He had horses in the north for twenty years with almost no success at all, but his outlook was such that he would shrug misfortune aside by saying, 'We'll get there one day.' After being introduced to us by Greville Starkey, he decided to have one horse a year in our stable, and thankfully his luck changed. Fabvista, who had been second in the Jersey Stakes at Royal Ascot, won him the Bunbury Cup on the July Course in 1973, and then in 1977 Countess Lor, a bay filly by Lorenzaccio, won at Wolverhampton, Leicester and Newbury before breaking her leg at Goodwood. As a replacement for Countess Lor we paid 2,500 guineas on his behalf for Connaught Bridge, who won the Nassau Stakes (£17,730) at Goodwood and then realized a dream of a lifetime for Herbert with her success in the Yorkshire Oaks (£28,620) at York, his favourite racecourse.

Soon after the triumphs of Connaught Bridge Herbert was taken ill. At that time he had a chestnut colt called Barwin with us. Barwin was a tough, cheeky individual, and we used to joke that Herbert must have shown much the same traits as a young man. In the end Barwin became too much of a handful, and we had to cut him.

Herbert was a forthright man and a bit of a rough diamond, who always called a spade a shovel. He loved champagne, and many a happy time we had in a racecourse bar with him. I was very glad that his family took over Barwin after his death, as the horse won five times as a three-year-old in 1981. The old man's ashes were sprinkled around the winning-post at York.

Most enthusiastic of my owners must be a remarkable man from Khartoum, by the name of Souren Vanian. Large and portly, he has a zest for living in proportion to his ample frame. One of the pictures in his family album of which he is proudest shows him kicking a football with the Scottish International player Alan Brazil, and one cannot but remark upon the contrasting physiques. Mr Vanian had a two-year-old called Laurette in training at Warren Place in 1982, and is currently building up a collection of bloodstock at the Derisley Wood Stud at Newmarket.

We are lucky to have an owner like millionaire Paris art dealer Daniel Wildenstein, who can always be relied upon to supply the stable with high-class horses from the fifty-odd broodmares on his studs. Louis Freedman, who is the deputy senior steward of the Jockey Club, is another successful owner. He has the Cliveden Stud near Maidenhead. So far his fillies have tended to be rather better than his colts. Among the good horses that we have trained for him has been Royal Hive (by Royal Palace), who won the Park Hill Stakes at Doncaster in 1977.

Nicky Phillips, another of my owners, is related by marriage, as his sister Fiona is the wife of my brother Jamie. He inherited the racing interests of his grandparents, Sir Harold and Lady Zia Wernher. Sir Harold Wernher, who died in 1973, owned Brown Jack, one of the most popular horses of the 1930s and winner of Royal Ascot's Queen Alexandra Stakes six years running, and later in life Aggressor, successful in the King George VI and the Queen Elizabeth Stakes at Ascot in 1960. Lady Zia Wernher, the daughter of a Russian Grand Duke, was eighty-five when she died in 1977. She had a long and successful association with Uncle Cecil, who began it by buying Double Life for 600 guineas as a yearling in 1927. Not only did Double Life win the Cambridgeshire but she became the foundation mare of Lady Zia's Someries Stud, and great-granddam of Meld, whom Uncle Cecil trained to win the 1,000 Guineas, the Oaks and the St Leger when I was a twelve-year-old prep-school boy in 1955.

A very tall man, Nicky Phillips is so quiet that you could almost call him shy, but one finds him a most intelligent conversationalist when one gets to know him. He lives on the family estate at Luton Hoo in Bedfordshire, and has built up a stud which he is continually improving by acquiring new bloodlines.

Julie and I are well aware of how much we owe to our owners. For the most part they have been a constant source of support, whether their horses have been winning Group races or proving bitter disappointments. I count my blessings and realize that in a lot of ways I have been spoiled by having the benefit of their understanding of horses, and dread the day that I have to train without their like. As I said earlier, it is ultimately the horses that are the sufferers when you train for owners who are in total ignorance of their nature.

# 8
## *The Professionals*

I am in no position to make a judgment on either jockeys or on my colleagues in the training profession, but there are certain individuals in both categories whom I have always admired.

Not surprisingly, the jockeys whom I hold in highest esteem are the three that have ridden my horses regularly, firstly while we were at the Marriott Stables and then after our move to Warren Place.

Joe Mercer was a wonderfully conscientious stable jockey in the mould of his father-in-law Harry Carr, who rode for the Captain for so many years. He is a true professional and a very stylish rider, who keeps his horses so perfectly balanced that they always run for him. He was retained by us the year that he became Champion, 1979, and deserved to be acclaimed as a truly great one, as he was absolutely brilliant. At forty-four he was by no means a young man in years, but very much one at heart, and proved himself a real master of his craft by his handling of Kris, Light Cavalry, Le Moss and Buckskin, to name just four of the winners that he rode for us that season.

He has a naughty, childlike sense of humour, and I found it difficult to know him at first, but in time a deep friendship and understanding developed between us. Whenever he is in the Newmarket area he still comes to have breakfast at Warren Place and rides out. Moreover, we continue to engage him to ride our horses whenever possible now that he is first jockey to Peter Walwyn.

Greville Starkey became our stable jockey in 1970 after he had been riding for John Oxley for a number of years. As well as being a fine race rider, and one of the best judges of pace of the present time, he is a superb horseman, which is by no means the same thing as a jockey. Our association was extremely successful, and he rode me my first classic winner when successful in the Irish 1,000 Guineas on that lovely filly, Cloonagh, owned and bred by my half-brother Arthur in 1973. It goes without saying that Julie and I were as much delighted by his winning the Derby on Shirley Heights in 1978 as we have been by the enormous success he has had since becoming first jockey to the powerful stable of Guy Harwood, for whom he won the 2,000 Guincas on To-Agori-Mou in 1981 and brought off the double on Kalaglow in the Eclipse Stakes and the King George VI and the Queen Elizabeth Diamond Stakes in 1982.

As well as much of our early success, Greville provided us with a great deal of amusement. I shall never forget the aftermath of his winning on Katie Cecil at Deauville in August 1973. He had been wasting to ride light, and on the way back from France we decided to celebrate by dining at The Mirabelle in Curzon Street, the party consisting of Katie Cecil's owner Lord Dunraven, Tote Cherry-Downes – who was then managing the Fort Union Stud for him in Ireland – Greville, Julie and myself. Lord Dunraven chose the most expensive wine in the house, which was about £50 a bottle, and Greville, not having had much to eat for several days, was soon in tremendous form. Half-way through dinner he began doing his well-known imitation of a dog, barking very loudly, like a guard greeting an intruder – R-r-ruff! R-r-ruff!

The clientele of The Mirabelle did not seem accustomed to this kind of impromptu performance, and the other four of us were made to feel rather embarrassed. I remember seeing Sir Charles Clore, looking very far from amused. We therefore paid the bill very quickly, while the 'R-r-ruff, R-r-ruff' continued in the background, and proceeded to take our leave of the establishment. There was a long napkin on our table, and I rolled it into a loop before putting it around Greville's neck as a lead, then going down on all fours he barked his way out of the door. And he ruff r-r-ruffed it all the way home to Newmarket too.

Like everybody else, Julie and I admire Lester Piggott tremendously. He is as great a genius as there is to be found in any walk of life at the present time. He is the truly dedicated professional for whom nothing is too much trouble if it will bring him another winner. His natural weight is very much greater than that of the average jockey, but he has controlled it by stringent dieting for many years, and I think that he has reached the stage where this dieting comes so naturally to him that it no longer presents him with a problem. He does not have a particularly highly developed taste for sophisticated food in any case, and quite often ends a day of fasting by climbing into the car, clutching three ice-cream cornets, after racing.

Lester has a very interesting face. I think it looks more relaxed, and he enjoys life more, now that he has settled into a job near to his Newmarket home, instead of continually flying backwards and forwards to fulfil commitments in Ireland. People say that Lester seldom smiles, but that is not true. He has a wickedly dry sense of humour, but rather than show his appreciation of a joke by baring his teeth in a grin like that of a circus clown, his amusement is revealed in those eternally alert blue eyes. Lester is also said to be hard of hearing. I have never found that to be the case, and have never had to repeat anything. The truth is that Lester hears what he wants to hear.

He loves to come to Warren Place after racing, or on a Sunday, when he is completely relaxed, and we sit and chat for hours. Sometimes it gets so late into the evening that I say, 'Lester, I'll see you in the morning. I must go and have a bath before dinner.'

'What do you mean? I'm staying for dinner!' is not infrequently the reply.

Lester and I get on extraordinarily well, and understand each other. I have always had the impression that he cannot decide whether or not I am the village idiot, but I think we have a lot of respect for each other. I certainly have for him.

He performs his duties as stable jockey impeccably. Even if he has been to a dinner in London the previous evening, he is always available to ride first lot. On the racecourse he is phenomenal, and not just on the big occasions: no race is too small to bring out the best in him. His strength in a finish is quite remarkable, and Julie and I, who have known him for a long time, think that he is riding better than ever. We are honoured by having him attached to Warren Place, and look forward to the association lasting for many more seasons.

Of my fellow-trainers I have a particularly high opinion of John Dunlop, a personal friend, who does consistently well each season, the royal trainer Major Dick Hern, whose record speaks for itself, and Michael Stoute, whose rise to the top of his profession is quite remarkable considering that he did not arrive in this country until 1965, after being born and brought up in Barbados, where his father was a Commissioner of Police.

# 9
# *All in a Day's Work*

There seems to be a popular misconception that a racehorse trainer does little more than stand in the paddock, smoking a large cigar, giving incomprehensible orders to a deaf jockey and then drinking and dining with millionaire owners. Such ideas do trainers very much less than justice, as our life is a long way from being a perpetual social round. It is not without significance that the Craven Club and the Subscription Rooms, once the two most fashionable clubs in Newmarket, both regarded trainers as the backbone of their membership, and both have been obliged to close their doors. The fact is that recent multiplication of paperwork and administrative duties just does not leave the modern trainer time to go to his club for a drink before lunch and dinner in the way that his predecessor did.

At the same time as being rewarding and enjoyable, the training profession is as demanding as Uncle Cecil warned me it would be, and preparing and entering the horses for their races is just part of one's work. In addition one has to keep owners informed of the progress of their horses, entertain them on their visits to the stable, fulfil one's responsibilities as an employer of staff, attend to the buying and selling of horses, ensure that the stables and ancillary buildings are properly maintained, and do one's best to satisfy the legitimate curiosity of the racing Press. In many ways the trainer is one of the Public Relations Officers of a large and complex industry, and if there is a bit of the psychologist about him so much the better, as he needs to understand people as well as horses.

Some people are horrified at the idea of getting up early

in the morning, but I find it no hardship as I do not know what it is like to lie in bed until eight or nine, thereby missing what in many ways is the best part of the day. I love the early morning. When I get up shortly before six o'clock everything is so peaceful, and the air is so pure.

The only disadvantage to early rising is that acceptance of an invitation to dinner makes it a long day. By late evening one tends to become drowsy, and that can result in it being hard to make oneself agreeable to one's neighbour at table.

Having let in the cats and let out the dogs, Buckskin, the black Labrador, and Naughty Nancy (a mixture of almost everything else), as soon as I come downstairs in the morning, I try to arrange my thoughts on what is to be done during the day ahead while having three cups of coffee and as many cigarettes during the three-quarters of an hour until 6.50. I find the two hours between six and eight in the morning the best time of the day for working. One's brain is at its freshest, and one is quite free from interruption – until Katie appears wanting help with her homework or her goldfish bowl moved nearer the sink so that she can change the water. During those couple of hours I open my post, make a final check on my list of which lad is to ride which horse, put in half an hour or so entering the horses for their races, or phone one or two people before they leave for the City so that they will not have to try to ring me in the evening when the phone is off the hook.

At 6.50 I put on my moccasins and go out into the yard with my riding-out board, into which the names of the horses are slotted on one side and those of the lads riding that morning the other. The staff van arrives from the town at about seven o'clock, but many of the lads like to come up independently rather earlier so that they will not be rushed.

While the lads are mucking out two or three boxes

apiece I see Paddy Rudkin to find out whether any horse has left its feed from the previous evening, as he will have been round all the horses before they had their first feed of the day. If he is not happy about one of them we look it over together to decide what is to be done. After that I go through the same procedure with Dodger Hooper in the fillies' yard and then return to the house to make another cup of coffee and take a not particularly palatable multi-vitamin pill.

My decision as to what the horses wear at first lot necessarily depends upon the weather. If it is warm they wear light sheets. If it is on the cool side they wear the heavier rugs. At eight o'clock first lot pulls out of the yard, colts in front of the string, fillies at the back. When at full strength first lot consists of fifty horses, mostly the older ones and just a handful of the more forward two-year-olds already in serious training.

Most other trainers have their strings on the Heath much earlier than ours, and the boxes are probably mucked out on return. However, I do not think that ambling around in the half-light of early morning is beneficial to the horses, or particularly enjoyable for the lads. By the time we start work the sun is up, while any overnight frost there might have been is usually out of the ground. I believe that all horses appreciate warmth, and it is not only fillies that need to feel the sun on their backs. Another advantage of coming on to the Heath when we do is that it is less crowded than earlier on, and there is less likelihood of the string having to take a turn or two by walking round in a circle while we wait for another string to go up the canter or gallop that we are going to use.

In my opinion it is absolutely essential for a trainer to ride out with his string. It enables one to get to know each horse better than ever, and I have often been struck how much more one can often learn from watching a horse walking along than from seeing it galloping. Driving up in a car to meet the string on the working ground deprives one of the opportunity to make such a close observation.

Almost every successful trainer I have ever known has ridden out with his horses, and most trainers' wives are also generally closely involved in the running of the stable. Julie, for instance, rides out two lots every day, and the training of horses has been a way of life for her from earliest childhood. I find it not only a pleasure but also a great practical asset to be able to discuss with her the traits of the horses and the way they are coming along when we are alone together, and cannot imagine how trainers manage when their wives are not as much immersed in horses as they are themselves. By the same token it must be incredibly boring for a woman to be married to a trainer if she has very little interest in racing, or only cares for the social side of it.

It is impossible to generalize about methods of training, as there is such a huge difference in the requirements of various horses. They work over different distances, and some (endowed with strong constitutions) need a lot of work to get them fit and keep them straight for racing, while others, who are less robust, need very little galloping to bring them to the peak of condition. By and large the horses gallop twice a week, Wednesdays and Saturdays, when Lester Piggott is on hand to ride as many as half a dozen of them in their faster paces. On other days the string is confined to routine cantering to keep the horses fit and healthy.

On galloping mornings we ascertain a horse's current form or explore its potential by setting it a harder task or sending it a longer distance than hitherto, as well as putting the finishing touches to getting them fit a few days before running. It can take as long as two hours' work the previous evening to prepare the schedules for galloping mornings, as it is important to have the weights and distances right. Obviously one does not want to gallop two horses of approximately the same ability with one ridden by a heavy lad of ten stone or more and the other ridden by a little apprentice of seven stone, as the one with the heavier weight will have a heart-breaking job. I like to swap them around because the lads become attached to the horses in their personal care, and the horses are clever enough to take advantage of anyone liable to be too easy with them by refusing to put their backs into their work.

After first lot I have breakfast with Paddy, and if I am leaving early to go racing, I plan the work to be done at second lot. As we fly to a good many meetings nowadays I am often able to supervise second lot myself, and do not leave the yard until 12.30. There is a charter service from Newmarket racecourse, which puts a great many courses within easy reach, and we can be at Newbury, for instance, in thirty-five minutes.

Because of all the time it saves, flying is a real god-send. Motoring, on the other hand, is becoming more difficult, with the roads seeming to get more congested every day, and can be very tiring. This is especially the case at weekends, when on returning from the Park courses in the London area – Sandown and Kempton – we meet the traffic coming out of the City on Friday evenings. With so much travelling by road unavoidable, it is essential to have a comfortable car. I no longer write off cars with the regularity that I did when doing fewer miles to the gin and lime than to a gallon of petrol. Since switching to Mercedes I have had fourteen without a scratch.

Like a lot of racing people, we have our superstitions. We never fill the petrol tank early in the day prior to going racing, as we have found it unlucky. Instead we buy petrol on the journey, having already laid in a large supply of jelly babies and fruit pastilles, and as often as not we will have collected Tote Cherry-Downes, whom we find as amusing as ever. As well as to Tote we listen to tapes, usually a Simon and Garfunkel cassette. Their *Bridge Over Troubled Water* is my favourite song.

Before leaving for the races I will have disposed of my most distasteful chore of the day, which is the quarter of an hour that has to be spent in the office.

Scrivvy, who has two girls to help her, copes with most things, but there are always one or two to which I have to attend every day. The office always frightens me. It seems full of computers and flashing lights, and there is the awful telephone. To me the telephone is symbolic of an angry owner giving vent to his feelings in unpleasantly measured terms, or the travelling head lad ringing from a distant course to report that a fancied runner has hurt himself or has a temperature. No wonder I hate it enough to leave it off the hook as often as possible, though I do have an ex-directory number for the family and for stable emergencies.

Dictation is my other great aversion. Whenever I have to write to an owner I scribble on a large pad, late at night or early in the morning. Scrivvy then deciphers these hieroglyphics (which I could never read back to myself) and composes a letter from them. It is amazing how much correspondence I can do in this way. Sometimes I have taken no more than half an hour to put a dozen two-sided letters on to my scribbling pad.

Most meetings to which we go by car take a couple of hours to reach, as I must admit that I do not go to the more distant ones unless I can fly. I like to arrive at the course early. I hate being pushed for time in which to get there, or, worse still, being late, and usually leave after the last of my horses has run.

Of the courses close to London I like Ascot and Sandown Park best, while Goodwood and Newbury are my favourite among the other southern courses. I do not like being away from Warren Place overnight more than necessary, but we usually stay away for the five days of the Goodwood July meeting and take the opportunity to relax in the beautiful Sussex countryside. Over the Newbury Spring meeting we spend a night with Lambourn trainer Paul Cole most years. As a sop to my conscience for being away from the stable I try to field a strong team of runners at both those meetings. This paid off particularly handsomely at Goodwood in 1979, when we had seven winners there.

At Sandown Julie and I make for the seafood bar on arrival, and take dishes of crawfish tails, or the like, to huddle in a corner to try to avoid being cross-questioned about the chances of our runners, as we so often are, by complete strangers. Being touted by people one does not know at all, or hardly knows, is one of the most unpleasant parts of going racing. There is nothing secretive about the way our stable is run, as the merits or otherwise of our horses are quickly established in public, and we co-operate with the Press as much as possible by keeping them informed about running plans and other things. Therefore I can hardly be expected to like being interrogated by punters eager for inside information on the walk from the stands to the weighing-room to check with the travelling head lad that our runners have arrived safely. Really all I can tell people is that the horses are only running because I think they have a chance.

As opposed to the touts, and those individuals who try to create the impression of being on the inside of racing by constantly approaching trainers, there are the regular racegoers, who always wish us well and seem to follow our horses all the time. We have become attached to a number of these people over the years, and have pet names for each of them. Doncaster would not be the same without 'Mr Cigar'. Always overjoyed when one of our horses wins, he likes to feel part of the team, and by way of celebration flicks a Havana cigar from his breast-pocket with the deftness of a magician producing a rabbit from a hat.

Another regular racegoer we call Mr Hyacinth. He works for a Dutch bulb firm, and often presents us with a mass of assorted bulbs for our garden.

At Yarmouth there is Mr Fish. He sends us lobster, crab, sole or turbot by the way of the travelling head lad, who thankfully brings the 'catch' home in the horse-box. I would hate to drive back to Newmarket in a car laden with fish at the height of summer.

Every now and again we come across an extremely rotund gentleman who needs some help in enabling a bookmaker solve his cash-flow. This is Mr Fruity. If we are able to assist him in resolving his problem he expresses his gratitude by presenting us with a crate of sour-looking apples, on top of a layer of thickskinned plums, all propped up by black, squashed bananas. I must look like a Covent Garden porter as I carry this offering around until finding somewhere to deposit it until after racing.

There are regular punters on every course who stop me to offer me a boiled sweet. I usually decline them. I was always taught not to accept sweets from strangers.

The people whom I dread most are the large, jolly East Enders, in their shiny suits and black trilbies, who put a vice-like grip on one's arm and say ''Ello, ''Ennery, 'ow nice to see you again!' I will never have seen them in my life before, and when three days later I am still nursing the bruises on my arm I sincerely hope I will never see them again.

Happily, we also have many good friends on the racecourses, including most of the gatemen. They are always pleased to see us, and when one of them is missing I generally inquire of his whereabouts. 'Don't worry,' one of his colleagues will reply. 'He's got 'flu, but he will be at Newmarket next week.'

It is sad, however, that some of the officials on the

lesser tracks do not seem to follow racing at all. On occasions when I have forgotten my trainer's badge I have had the greatest difficulty in gaining admission. It was not at a Group Three course that I suffered my most humiliating experience but at Ascot. Having left my badge on another suit, I was frogmarched away, and missed seeing an important race.

Although I enjoy the atmosphere of the racecourse, and meeting friends, I cannot really say I derive much pleasure from watching a race. I get very nervous before one of my horses runs, whether in a maiden race or a classic. There was a time when I was very grateful if the owner was abroad, so that I would have no explaining or comforting to do, but nowadays I appreciate the owner's interest in his horse, and like him to see the best, or the worst, for himself. People show their nerves in different ways. In my own case it is by constantly puffing at a cigarette from the time they go down to the start until the winner has passed the post. By then I really am quite exhausted, and almost drained of nervous energy. I would not have things any other way, for the day I am no longer nervous about my horses I will know that I have not enough interest in them to be able to train them properly.

I never use binoculars. This was originally because I would invariably leave them in the bars in the days of gin and lime. They are, of course, very expensive, and having lost four pairs in as many weeks, I decided, along with the insurance company, that it would be in my best interests to do without them. Over the years I have trained my eyes, and am amazed how far I can see on a racecourse. I can see the colours of my runners from as far as five furlongs out on the straight course at Newmarket, and can follow them well on any round course. Admittedly, when the field is as far as five furlongs away I cannot see whether my horse is going well or badly, pulling for his head or being pushed along, but at least I am spared being disconcerted by seeing him denied a clear run or being brought under heavy pressure as he struggles to keep his place. As far as I am concerned, the only part of a race that matters is the finish. As long as a horse comes through strongly in the final furlong the early stages of the race are irrelevant.

When planning programmes for the horses I rely on instinct to a very large extent, and spend less time on an analysis of the form-book than most people imagine. I do not deny that I sometimes stretch out on our eight-foot Chinese sofa and check on a horse when some details of his performances have slipped my memory, but I do feel that some people take the form-book too literally. If, for example, a horse of mine beats another by two lengths, and mine is 9lb worse off next time they meet, the students of the book will say the placings should be reversed, as a length is the equivalent to 3lb, so instead of being beaten by two lengths the other horse should win by one length. That is not necessarily the case. The horse I beat might have been at its peak, then lost its form in the meantime. My horse might have run green and needed the experience. The second might have had a clearer run than my horse, or my jockey might have ridden an indifferent race, whereas Lester rode the second. There are so many variables to be taken into account when assessing the value of a performance that one cannot apply hard-and-fast rules. If I think a horse of mine is fit and well I will send him out thinking he can win, no matter the disadvantage he is at according to the form-book, and very often he will win.

Seeing one's horse in the winner's enclosure is always exciting, though it is sometimes hard to inspect him as closely as one wants to do when surrounded by the Press. But they have a job to do, and I get on very well with them on the whole. Among the reporters are some very capable journalists, who understand racing, although I do feel that a section of them are sensationalists with the one word 'scoop' forever on their minds. I know that over-dramatizing racing, or anything else, can sell newspapers, but it is more satisfying to read journalists who know their racing and can recognize a good horse or a really fine piece of riding. To relegate a good performance on the part of a horse to the bottom of a column in order to give prominence to failure or the careless riding of a jockey is to get things right out of proportion. I was greatly upset by the Press's coverage of the success of Diesis in the Dewhurst Stakes in 1982. All the headlines of the following day announced the unexpected failure of Gorytus. Diesis, though, was winning his second Group One race in a fortnight, and deserved recognition.

After winning a race I am sometimes asked if I will be interviewed on television, and am usually happy to oblige. At first I was very nervous and did not like it at all, but I find those interviews quite enjoyable now. To begin with I talked too quickly, and could not resist the urge to look at myself on the monitor to see what I looked like on the box. These days I know there is plenty of time in which to formulate an answer to a question and the interviewer will wait for it. I know Julian Wilson of the BBC and Brough Scott of ITV very well, and appreciate that they would not put me in an awkward position or try to make a fool of me. I do not know how I come over in those interviews, but I am always anxious to play myself down by making it clear that it is the horse and the owner who deserve the credit. Taking too much credit for yourself is never advisable. Racing is a great leveller, and in the end one is always brought down to earth.

Jim Stanford, 'Captain Heath' of the *Daily Mail*, is the Pressman of whom I see most. He does a lot of public-relations work for Daniel Wildenstein, and is a great help in many ways. I admire his work, and he could not be a more honest, diligent person. Jim likes to relax over a drink at the end of a day, and very rarely over-indulges himself. I do remember one sales week here at Newmarket, though, when the Press were invited to dine with the Jockey Club. After a hard day's work Jim had a drink or two with Bill Marshall, who was then training in the town, in the early part of the evening. Arriving at the Jockey Club more than a little flushed, he practically dropped his head into the soup and was violently ill all over the carpet while making a desperate attempt to reach the door. With his frilly shirt-front the lurid hues of the first two courses, he made a gallant attempt to retrieve the situation by contributing to the informal debate that followed the dinner, only to find himself totally inarticulate for what must have been the only time in his life. Eventually Lord Howard de Walden brought proceedings to a close by saying, 'That concludes the evening, gentlemen. Unless there is anything else Mr Stanford wants to bring up!'

For a long time afterwards Jim was known as the Meat and Two Veg Vesuvius. I know it is a wicked story, but Jim has a great sense of humour and will see the funny side of it. As a journalist and a person there is no better.

Elsewhere in the media, Terry Wogan seems to find me a suitable subject in which to indulge his sense of humour. I have not yet forgiven him for reporting that I was seen on the Newmarket July course wearing a pair of trousers embroidered with ducks and an army surplus jacket one day in 1982. He was quite right about the trousers, but the jacket to which he referred was an extremely expensive suede garment.

Julie had met Wogan some twelve months before that broadcast when he presented her with a set of crystal glasses, which she was collecting on my behalf as a prize for having brought off most trebles that season. The little ceremony was completed very much more successfully than it had been when I received a similar prize two years earlier. Within minutes someone had dropped all the glasses on to a patch of concrete.

I am glad that I do not have to compete with the brilliant young northern trainer Michael Dickinson on the score of completing trebles, as he confines his activities to jumping. Unlike him, I am not a lover of National Hunt racing. Unaware that there was a steeplechase and a hurdle on the card at Newbury one day – because I thought that they had finished with mixed racing there the previous year – I remarked to a friend 'Hell! I thought they had done away with this game.' That remark was overheard by a reporter and duly appeared in the Press next day, doing nothing, I suppose, to endear me to my colleagues in the winter sport.

Some people train horses for the flat and jumpers with equal success, but I find concentration on the flat gives me quite enough to do for eleven months in the year. By the time we arrive home in the evening after a race meeting it will already be eight o'clock. The first thing I do is to see Paddy Rudkin to find out whether any problems have arisen. If a horse has pulled a tendon, or met with any other setback, we go out into the yard immediately to inspect the damage, as I could not sleep without seeing the extent of it for myself.

# 10
## *My Hobby-horses*

The more I have become involved in racing the more I have taken it upon myself to find other interests to take my mind off the pressures of the business temporarily. Until comparatively recently we just went flat out for eleven months of the year, our lives totally dominated by the horses, and recharged our batteries with a break each January. It has become clear to me over the years that to grind oneself into the ground like this is no good to anybody.

When one is young there is a tendency to forgo relaxation and recreation in favour of work. Ambition takes over from common sense. Plenty of people were forthcoming with words of advice like: 'Now you must settle down, otherwise you will burn youself out.' They were always received with a shrug or a smile. Not any more. They were quite right, of course. My profession is fairly demanding, and gives rise to a certain amount of stress and strain. The stable routine and the travelling make it a breakneck pace of life, and having had an ulcer operation in the early seventies I have got into a habit, on doctor's advice, of having a lazy hour stretched out on the sofa after lunch, with the telephone off the hook during the winter.

I am never allowed to forget, incidentally, that while I was in hospital the stable's percentage of winners spiralled! My midday forty winks have become such a habit that when the season starts I find it difficult to readjust. The awful thing is that I can sleep in any place at any time. Julie usually drives to the races while I nod off in the passenger seat.

It seemed like a good idea at the time to take up golf as a hobby. Julie had started to play one year on our holiday in Barbados. She would go off with the Newmarket-on-Sea crowd – parts of the West Indies are virtually taken over by the racing fraternity early each New Year – and fiddle around the nine-hole course in 200 strokes or more, having missed out the fifth because of the distance from the club house, and the heat. I could see I did not have much to beat, so I decided to try my hand as well.

We would have great fun after stables in the summer evenings, and we would always play a nice little course near Chester when staying in Cheshire for the races and again on our winter holiday. At great expense I bought myself a set of clubs which included a St Andrews putter complete with hickory shaft, and we started having regular lessons from the professional at Worlington, our local course. These coaching sessions bored me terribly, although the tutor was very good, and demonstrated great patience. At home we drove plastic balls, which go only a third of the distance that a normal golfball will travel, from a special pad, and my left-handed belts started to go a fair way after some practice. Julie, alas, got worse and worse. Her drives either went off at right angles into the Warren Place windows, or trickled pitifully a few feet in front of her instead of smashing down the daffodils and tulips at the far end of the garden.

One evening, after a particularly bad spell of near-drives, she stormed into the house in a fearful rage. And never played again. As I had only taken up the game to keep her company, I was quite put out. I had to hang up my new golf-bag and reluctantly start a dispersal sale of my irons and clubs. Our retirement did please one person, however. Gordon, the gardener, was relieved to see the standing down of the budding stars. It was not so much the ball doing the damage, rather the two pairs of feet trampling down everything in sight while retrieving it from all corners of the greenery.

It was after our exit from the golfing scene that we decided on a much more sedate hobby. Warren Place, with its masses of space, was the first home we had owned ourselves, and the idea evolved that we would become gardeners. Having set about improving the garden, we became a little more adventurous in our efforts to create something new. The vegetable garden had plenty of room for improvement, and we focused our attention on that. Practically every vegetable under the sun was put into the soil, and we even laid down no fewer than eleven asparagus beds. One of the strains of pea grown at Warren Place emanates, believe it or not, from the tomb of Tutankhamen. Then an orchard was brought in and we started to grow figs, melons and grapes in addition to the usual fruits.

But the master-stroke was to create quite a number of old-fashioned rose gardens while renewing the established one in front of the house. These displays bring us never-ending pleasure. The old-fashioned roses have become our main interest. We have had much fun over the past few years designing the gardens, making changes and improvements, and watching them burst into colour. We have become so obsessed that the rose displays have reached massive proportions, and we now require two full-time gardeners. It may be an expensive hobby, but we love it, and find it very relaxing. I can assure anyone who is not familiar with old-fashioned roses that they are missing Nature at its finest. The colours of species like the Bourbon, the Damask and the Rugosa with their hips and centifolias are so delicate, and the scents are out of this world. I find that the modern hybrid is almost vulgar in comparison with these beautiful flowers. Their colours are too gaudy, and they lack the beauty in the shape of the plants as well as the roses themselves.

Many of the old roses grow to great heights and widths, some of sprawling nature and others of tidy habit. The single roses are mainly descendants of the old Scottish briar. I think the rose, with such a history, and such splendour, is unrivalled by any other flower. Some of ours are summer-flowering, some recurring and others continuous. A number of our friends have become interested in our hobby, and we order roses for them. One day they will be getting as much pleasure from their gardens as we do. In our spare time we like nothing better than to wander round the roses, inspecting their progress and generally studying them. On a day when two favourites have been beaten and a horse has broken down on the gallops, for us to stroll leisurely round our garden is what it is like for a businessman to sit down to a game of backgammon in the Clermont Club and have his thoughts about City shares buried for a while.

Another of my interests, which I have probably inherited from my mother, is clothes. She thinks of little else, and has always been very well dressed. Even now she is usually draped in the latest fashions. I used to dress in a very flashy way. I would wear very brightly coloured patchwork trousers and white shoes at meetings like Glorious Goodwood and the July meeting at Newmarket, and I unfortunately became renowned for my outrageous tastes. One day Julie, squirming with embarrassment, was confronted by Mr Joel, who told her, 'All he needs is a banjo and he could join the Black and White Minstrels!' The only times I wear 'stage costumes' these days are while on holiday in the Caribbean and at home in the garden. I have come to like on the whole much more conservative clothes. Blue shirts, dark suits, herringbone sports jackets and grey trousers are now much more the order of the day. I like my clothes very well cut and insist on narrow trousers, while I still put on Gucci footwear of all descriptions.

I have a horrifyingly large wardrobe, with more than 150 shirts and some 100 pairs of shoes. Like most people, I have become attached to certain suits and shirts and tend to keep on wearing the same ones while the others just hang around. They always say that if you have not worn something for a year you should get rid of it because after such a lapse of time you will never put it on again. I adhere to this, and the beneficiaries are my gardener and my head man's son, who are the same size as me and now probably walk around better dressed than I do myself. My love of clothes prompted Julie and me to go into a business partnership in a boutique in Newmarket. At The Clothes Horse, with Nina Judd as our partner, we sell casual trousers and jeans of most good makes, along with shirts and sweaters. We would love to be able to shop around London for suits and different lines to sell, but we simply do not have the time. We do, however, get a lot of enjoyment out of the shop. I utterly refuse to let someone buy something unless I am totally satisfied that they look their best in it. The customer coming out of one of the cubicles in a pair of scarlet trousers that are too big in the backside will say, 'I will have these.' I invariably reply, 'No, you won't. They just do not fit, and you look awful in them.' After giving her a pair two sizes smaller she is thrilled with herself after a look in the mirror and leaves the shop well pleased.

I remember one very pretty girl who was having great difficulty in getting into her chosen pair of jeans. She shouted from the cubicle for help after she had lost the battle to pull the zip up, and Nina shouted back the reply that she would go in and give her a hand. 'No, I will,' I interjected. 'What do you think I have got this shop for!' Julie and I try to spend a few hours a week in the shop, although when racing is in full swing we have no chance. The shop only just makes a profit, and we would not like to try to live off the proceeds. But it is a nice diversion for us.

I have recently embarked on another business venture.

My brother David has been installed as manager of the Cliff Stud on the North Yorkshire moors near Helmsley, and we have formed a partnership with the aim of producing top-quality yearlings for the sales, with the help of Tote Cherry-Downes. Julie's parents ran the stud for more than thirty years, and we stepped in when they decided to give up the lease. In a short time it has been expanded to 250 acres, so there is plenty of room for the foals and yearlings, as well as the cattle and sheep.

Although food can be classed as one of my hobbies, drink – at least of the alcoholic variety – cannot. I have been teetotal for more than a decade. I have nothing against alcohol. It is simply that we do not suit each other. It used either to make me laugh uncontrollably or spur me into a bout of aggressive behaviour. And it was when I awoke one morning, bitterly regretting my action in telling an owner to take his horses away if he did not like the way I was training them, that I signed the pledge. I now get far more enjoyment out of a cup of tea than ever I did with a glass of something in my hand. If I am in a situation where it might be considered offensive to refuse a drink I may just stretch myself to a small shandy – two parts lemonade and one beer. But that is a rarity. I can just as easily clink a china cup to say: 'Cheers.'

I have had a great deal of fun writing this book, and it is unfortunate that one just does not remember all the many humorous things that happen over the years. There are probably quite a few stories that would have added to the tale's appeal, but as I have forgotten them it is as well that I have put pen to paper now, and not left it for another twenty years, when senility will probably be creeping in. Another reason for not delaying the book until then is that few people might want to read it come the turn of the century! To sum up, I would like to say that racing has been good to us, and Julie and I and our friends have had a great many thrills out of it so far. It is our way of life, and my only hope is that it does not become ruined through racing as a sport gradually being replaced by racing as an industry. As for the future, I will go on as long as I have enthusiasm for, and enjoyment from, the racing game. The ambition must remain there, too, for without it one is no longer competitive, while I could never be content to be an also-ran. It would be lovely to win the Derby one day, but that has never been my greatest dream. To run a powerful and successful stable which is respected by the racing fraternity, and to keep it at that standard, is as much as I ever dare ask for. Let me sign off with my home-made recipe for success. Find something you love doing. Make it a way of life. Work unceasingly at making a go of it, and this simple message will come filtering through: success is a far better bet than failure.

# Appendix

## *Henry Cecil's Statistical Record 1969–84*

By Phillip Smith

N.B.

(a) Races Abroad are indicated by the *symbol.

(b) Although the Pattern Race system was not introduced until 1971, races won in 1969 and 1970 which subsequently received Group status have been included.

**Analysis**

Statistically, Henry Cecil's training career can be divided into three broad areas.

(a) Initially there was the 'ivy up a wall' period when, from 1969 to 1974, a total of only 15 Pattern Race successes were recorded from a stable which averaged 73 inmates each year. Nevertheless, 20 per cent of all runners during this time were victorious, and on three occasions Cecil finished in the top ten in the Trainers' Table, which was a more than creditable start for a young trainer.

(b) 'The Italian connection', which flourished from 1975 to 1977, saw 21 Pattern Race victories thanks, to a large extent, to the exploits of Wollow and Bolkonski. The size of the stable increased to an average of 92 horses and 25 per cent of all runners were winners. In each year Cecil finished in the top ten of Winning Trainers, and in 1976 became Champion Trainer for the first time.

(c) The last seven years, 'Warren Place era', have seen Cecil establish himself as the most successful trainer in British racing. The number of horses housed at Warren Place has increased to an average of 134, three more English Classics have been won and he has been Champion Trainer on four occasions and runner up twice. During this time 34 per cent of all runners have been successful. 113 Pattern races have been won and the stable has grossed more than £6 million in total prize money. This has also been the most rewarding spell for followers of the stable, as it has brought a pre-tax profit of £1,400 at SP to a £10 level stake.

The comments below refer to the statistical tables which appear on subsequent pages.

**Table A:** By the end of the 1984 season Cecil had earned for his owners more than £5 million in first prize money and in excess of £6.5 million in win and place money. He had achieved 1,200 winners in the shortest time in British racing history, at a strike rate of 28 per cent. In terms of prize-money 1982 was his best season, although he trained more winners in 1979. He has been Champion Trainer on four occasions out of only sixteen as a trainer, and he has also trained more than a hundred winners in five seasons.

**Table B:** The stable has won a total of 149 Pattern Races, 144 at home and 5 abroad, of which 29 have been in Group 1 races. Interestingly, more than one-third of all these successes have been obtained by horses aged four and above. This figure, linked with the fact that 38 Pattern Races have been won by horses which joined Cecil after the end of their two-year-old careers, indicates the tremendous improvement he is able to bring about in older horses. He has a particularly good record in the Dante Stakes, the Futurity Stakes and the Nell Gwyn

Stakes, each of which he has won five times, the latter including four consecutive seasons. The Goodwood Cup, the Doncaster Cup and the Ascot Gold Cup have all been won on four occasions, the latter in consecutive years and the Queen Anne Stakes in each of the last four years. The figure of 24 successes gained in 1982 is a British record, beating the previous best of 23 set in 1979 also by Cecil.

**Table C:** July is traditionally the most prolific month for winners among the top trainers and the Henry Cecil stable is no exception, although in recent years August and September have also been successful months for the stable. May is the best month for older horses generally, although they are more likely to score in Group races in June. The three-year-olds appear to win consistently through the year until October, although the incidence of their victories in Pattern Races recedes after June. It is not until September and October that the two-year-olds are likely to win these races. Indeed Pushy and Precocious are the stable's only successes in Pattern Races for two-year-olds at Royal Ascot.

**Table D:** Henry Cecil has trained winners on all current British racecourses which are used for flat racing, although more than one in four of his successes have been achieved at Newmarket and Yarmouth. However Ascot, mainly due to the Royal meeting, has seen the majority of his wins in Group races. Although he has recorded 31 overall wins at both the Newmarket Craven meeting and at Royal Ascot, just nine have been achieved at the York Ebor meeting. The fact that 119 of his winners at Newmarket have come in the last seven years further illustrates the rise in the fortunes of the stable from 1978 onwards.

**Table E:** More than 50 different jockeys have ridden winners for the stable, with Joe Mercer and Lester Piggott leading the way with more than half of the successes between them. They have been even more dominant in Pattern Races, scoring on 80 per cent of the winners.

**Table F:** Statistically, Ardross probably just shades out Kris as the most successful horse trained by Cecil up to the end of 1984. Ardross won more money, and the greater number of graded races, whereas Kris won more races overall and had a higher ratio of wins and places to races run. Evidence of the impact of inflation on racing is the fact that although Bolkonski won two Group 1 races (including a Classic) as recently as 1975, his first-prize money total of £64,758 does not place him anywhere near the top ten of horses under the care of Cecil. However, Adonijah (who won two Group 3 races) is placed ninth because of minor wins and Group places.

**Table G:** Many of Henry Cecil's leading owners have had horses with him since the early 1970s, so that in terms of prize-money and races won Carlo d'Alessio, Charles St George, Lord Howard de Walden and Jim Joel figure highly. However, as Daniel Wildenstein has had horses at Warren Place for under seven seasons, the total of 123 winners is particularly noteworthy. Of the newer owners, the successes of Stavros Niarchos and particularly Sheikh Mohammed reflect their overall importance in British racing.

**Table H:** The list of leading sires of the horses trained by Henry Cecil is most revealing, with Sharpen Up and Habitat consistently figuring near the top of the categories researched. Remarkably, Sharpen Up's progeny have won on 64 per cent of times they have represented the stable, and have been placed on 87 per cent of their runs. Habitat has provided the stable with five individual winners of Group races, all of them fillies, in Roussalka, Home on the Range, Petroleuse, Strigida and Chalon.

**Table I:** A £10 level stake bet on every Henry Cecil runner since he started training has provided a pre-tax profit. Over the last seven years the profit is over £1,400, despite the bookmakers' increasingly cautious attitude to Warren Place horses and the trainers particularly open policy with the press.

**Table J:** Nowadays the official handicapper is particularly severe on horses trained at Warren Place. The number of successes in handicaps in 1984 was only two more than in 1969, yet the average weight carried by these horses was 9st 1lbs, compared with 8st 2lbs in 1969. Of course, Cecil enters better-quality horses in handicaps compared with other stables, though it does seem surprising that only one in nine of his 1984 winners came in handicaps. Furthermore, the strike rate in these races was only 21 per cent whereas overall it was 31 per cent.

**Table K:** The frequency of winners to runners on their seasonal debut further illustrates the dramatic 'take-off' in the fortunes of the stable which occurred in 1978. From 1969 to 1977 inclusive, 16 per cent of all seasonal debutants won. But from 1978 onward this figure has almost doubled to 31 per cent.

**Table L:** In the unlikely event of an older horse from the stable making his debut as late as October, back it. Cecil has a 100 per cent record in this area since 1969. July is the best month for seasonal debutants among the three-year-olds, while April and May are the months for two-year-olds. Yet again an overall profit has been obtained from a £10 level stake on all runners first time out since 1969, while the profit is more than £1,200 over the last seven years.

**Table A**
Yearly Analysis 1969–84

| *Year* | *Horses* | *Races* | *Wins* | % *Wins* | *Seconds* | *Thirds* | % *Placed* | *First Money* | *Total Money* |
|---|---|---|---|---|---|---|---|---|---|
| 1969 | 38 | 145 | 27 | 19% | 17 | 21 | 45% | £ 60,561.45 | £ 66,950.35 |
| 1970 | 51 | 206 | 35 | 17% | 30 | 17[1]* | 40% | 29,642.60 | 39,552.55 |
| | | | | | | | | | * 1,804.00 |
| 1971 | 61 | 239 | 53 | 22% | 38 | 28 | 50% | 52,354.15 | 75,780.00 |
| 1972 | 66 | 253 | 51[2]* | 21% | 38[1]* | 27[1]* | 47% | 45,698.80 | 67,962.40 |
| | | | | | | | | * 18,462.20 | * 23,245.20 |
| 1973 | 57 | 215 | 39[2]* | 19% | 33 | 31[1]* | 49% | 36,342.00 | 49,834.15 |
| | | | | | | | | * 23,883.30 | * 25,873.30 |
| 1974 | 64 | 260 | 50 | 19% | 37[1]* | 27 | 44% | 69,972.40 | 90,769.73 |
| | | | | | | | | | * 2,091.52 |
| 1975 | 74 | 293 | 82 | 28% | 60 | 31 | 59% | 205,428.47 | 241,741.92 |
| 1976 | 62 | 227 | 52 | 23% | 30[1]* | 33 | 51% | 261,500.64 | 809,377.06 |
| | | | | | | | | | * 14,084.00 |
| 1977 | 81 | 317 | 74 | 20% | 64[1]* | 35 | 55% | 169,918.70 | 245,509.37 |
| | | | | | | | | | * 28,169.01 |
| 1978 | 89 | 344 | 109[1]* | 32% | 69[3]* | 35[1]* | 63% | 382,350.70 | 555,400.28 |
| | | | | | | | | * 8,685.24 | * 26,865.46 |
| 1979 | 74 | 287 | 128 | 45% | 49[1]* | 23 | 70% | 683,880.80 | 809,377.06 |
| | | | | | | | | | * 14,084.00 |
| 1980 | 94 | 314 | 84[1]* | 27% | 53[1]* | 37[1]* | 56% | 460,104.80 | 604,147.25 |
| | | | | | | | | * 14,354.72 | * 25,392.24 |
| 1981 | 96 | 292 | 107[1]* | 37% | 44 | 32 | 63% | 588,558.05 | 709,254.51 |
| | | | | | | | | * 32,287.00 | * 35,515.00 |
| 1982 | 96 | 321 | 111 | 35% | 47[1]* | 38 | 61% | 872,619.60 | 1,022,990.17 |
| | | | | | | | | | * 67,227.00 |
| 1983 | 104 | 280 | 92 | 33% | 51 | 37 | 64% | 440,227.60 | 634,713.65 |
| | | | | | | | | | * 2,745.00 |
| 1984 | 108 | 352 | 108 | 31% | 75[1]* | 46[2]* | 66% | 551,877.05 | 747,663.81 |
| | | | | | | | | | * 21,452.66 |
| *Total* | 710 | 4,345 | 1,202[7]* | 28% | 735[11]* | 498[7]* | 57% | £4,911,037.81 | £6,250,402.14 |
| | | | | | | | | * 97,672,46 | * 279,019.39 |
| | | | | | | | | 5,008,710.27 | 6,529,421.53 |

*=Races Abroad.
[1]=(+1)
[2]=(+2)
[3]=(+3)
[5]=(+5)
[7]=(+7)
[10]=(+10)

**Table B**
Pattern race winners 1969–84

|  |  | | |
|---|---|---|---|
| 1969 | 2* | (including 2 at Group 1) | |
| 1970 | 2* | | |
| 1971 | 1 | | |
| 1972 | $3^{+}1$ | | (including $^{+}1$ at Group 1) |
| 1973 | $1^{+}1$ | | (including $^{+}1$ at Group 1) |
| 1974 | 4 | | |
| 1975 | 8 | (including 4 at Group 1) | |
| 1976 | 9 | (including 4 at Group 1) | |
| 1977 | 4 | | |
| 1978 | $14^{+}1$ | (including 1 at Group 1) | |
| 1979 | 23 | (including 5 at Group 1) | |
| 1980 | $13^{+}1$ | (including 2 at Group 1) | |
| 1981 | $14^{+}1$ | (including 3 at Group 1) | (including $^{+}1$ at Group 1) |
| 1982 | 24 | (including 4 at Group 1) | |
| 1983 | 12 | | |
| 1984 | 10 | (including 1 at Group 1) | |
| TOTAL | $144^{+}5$ | (including 26 at Group 1) | (including $^{+}3$ at Group 1) |

a) Although the Pattern race system was not introduced until 1971, races won in 1969 and 1970 which subsequently received Group race status have been included, and are marked by the * symbol.
b) Races abroad are indicated by the $^{+}$ symbol.

**Table B** (*cont*) Pattern Race Record 1969–84

| *Year* | *Age Group* | *Horses* | *Races* | *Wins* | *% Wins* | *Seconds* | *Thirds* | *% Placed* |
|---|---|---|---|---|---|---|---|---|
| 1969 | Older Horses | 1 | 3 | 1 | 33% | 1 | – | 67% |
| | 3 Year Olds | 1 | 1 | – | – | – | – | – |
| | 2 Year Olds | 1 | 1 | 1 | 100% | – | – | 100% |
| | *Total* | *3* | *5* | *2* | *40%* | *1* | – | *60%* |
| 1970 | Older Horses | 2 | 4 | 1 | 25% | 1 | 1 | 75% |
| | 3 Year Olds | 4 | 6 | 1 | 17% | – | – | 17% |
| | 2 Year Olds | 1 | 2 | – | – | – | 2 | 100% |
| | *Total* | *7* | *12* | *2* | *17%* | *1* | *3* | *50%* |
| 1971 | Older Horses | 2 | 3 | – | – | 1 | – | 33% |
| | 3 Year Olds | 4 | 6 | – | – | 1 | 1 | 33% |
| | 2 Year Olds | 1 | 1 | 1 | 100% | – | – | 100% |
| | *Total* | *7* | *10* | *1* | *10%* | *2* | *1* | *40%* |
| 1972 | Older Horses | 4 | 10 | 4 | 40% | – | 3 | 70% |
| | 3 Year Olds | 4 | 4 | – | – | – | – | – |
| | 2 Year Olds | 1 | 1 | – | – | 1 | – | 100% |
| | *Total* | *9* | *15* | *4* | *27%* | *1* | *3* | *53%* |
| 1973 | Older Horses | 1 | 3 | – | – | 1 | 1 | 67% |
| | 3 Year Olds | 9 | 14 | 2 | 14% | 2 | 2 | 43% |
| | 2 Year Olds | – | – | – | – | – | – | – |
| | *Total* | *10* | *17* | *2* | *12%* | *3* | *3* | *47%* |
| 1974 | Older Horses | 4 | 15 | 3 | 20% | 2 | 1 | 40% |
| | 3 Year Olds | 5 | 10 | – | – | 2 | 2 | 40% |
| | 2 Year Olds | 3 | 4 | 1 | 25% | – | – | 25% |
| | *Total* | *12* | *29* | *4* | *14%* | *4* | *3* | *38%* |
| 1975 | Older Horses | 5 | 11 | – | – | 3 | 2 | 45% |
| | 3 Year Olds | 7 | 17 | 5 | 29% | 2 | 1 | 47% |
| | 2 Year Olds | 8 | 11 | 3 | 27% | 1 | 2 | 54% |
| | *Total* | *20* | *39* | *8* | *21%* | *6* | *5* | *49%* |

**Table B** (*cont*) Pattern Race Record 1969–84

| | | | | | | | | |
|---|---|---|---|---|---|---|---|---|
| 1976 | Older Horses | 3 | 8 | 1 | 12% | – | – | 12% |
| | 3 Year Olds | 10 | 29 | 8 | 28% | 4 | 2 | 48% |
| | 2 Year Olds | 3 | 4 | – | – | – | 1 | 25% |
| | *Total* | *16* | *41* | *9* | *22%* | *4* | *3* | *39%* |
| 1977 | Older Horses | 6 | 16 | 2 | 12% | 1 | 1 | 25% |
| | 3 Year Olds | 7 | 17 | 2 | 12% | 5 | 2 | 53% |
| | 2 Year Olds | 1 | 1 | – | – | – | – | – |
| | *Total* | *14* | *34* | *4* | *12%* | *6* | *3* | *38%* |
| 1978 | Older Horses | 8 | 25 | 7 | 28% | 7 | 2 | 64% |
| | 3 Year Olds | 8 | 17 | 4 | 24% | 2 | 3 | 53% |
| | 2 Year Olds | 8 | 12 | 4 | 33% | 3 | 2 | 75% |
| | *Total* | *24* | *54* | *15* | *48%* | *12* | *7* | *63%* |
| 1979 | Older Horses | 2 | 5 | 4 | 80% | 1 | – | 100% |
| | 3 Year Olds | 12 | 43 | 16 | 37% | 7 | 4 | 63% |
| | 2 Year Olds | 5 | 7 | 3 | 43% | 1 | – | 57% |
| | *Total* | *19* | *55* | *23* | *42%* | *9* | *4* | *65%* |
| 1980 | Older Horses | 6 | 16 | 4 | 25% | 2 | 1 | 44% |
| | 3 Year Olds | 11 | 24 | 5 | 21% | 4 | 3 | 50% |
| | 2 Year Olds | 6 | 14 | 5 | 36% | – | 4 | 64% |
| | *Total* | *23* | *54* | *14* | *26%* | *6* | *8* | *52%* |
| 1981 | Older Horses | 5 | 17 | 8 | 47% | 1 | – | 53% |
| | 3 Year Olds | 9 | 16 | 6 | 37% | 1 | 2 | 56% |
| | 2 Year Olds | 10 | 14 | 1 | 7% | 3 | 4 | 57% |
| | *Total* | *24* | *47* | *15* | *32%* | *5* | *6* | *55%* |
| 1982 | Older Horses | 4 | 20 | 8 | 40% | 3 | 4 | 75% |
| | 3 Year Olds | 13 | 38 | 10 | 26% | 3 | 5 | 47% |
| | 2 Year Olds | 6 | 10 | 6 | 60% | – | – | 60% |
| | *Total* | *23* | *68* | *24* | *35%* | *6* | *9* | *57%* |

**Table B** (*cont*) Pattern Race Record 1969–84

| | | | | | | | | |
|---|---|---|---|---|---|---|---|---|
| 1983 | Older Horses | 4 | 10 | 3 | 30% | 3 | 1 | 70% |
| | 3 Year Olds | 14 | 27 | 4 | 15% | 2 | 7 | 48% |
| | 2 Year Olds | 5 | 11 | 5 | 45% | 1 | 3 | 82% |
| | *Total* | *23* | *48* | *12* | *25%* | *6* | *11* | *60%* |
| 1984 | Older Horses | 5 | 14 | 3 | 21% | 4 | 3 | 81% |
| | 3 Year Olds | 11 | 20 | 4 | 25% | 7 | 2 | 65% |
| | 2 Year Olds | 9 | 12 | 3 | 25% | 3 | – | 50% |
| | *Total* | *25* | *46* | *10* | *22%* | *14* | *5* | *63%* |
| Total | Older Horses | 62 | 180 | 49 | 27% | 31 | 20 | 56% |
| | 3 Year Olds | 129 | 289 | 67 | 23% | 42 | 36 | 50% |
| | 2 Year Olds | 68 | 105 | 33 | 31% | 13 | 18 | 61% |
| | *Overall Total* | *259* | *574* | *149* | *26%* | *86* | *74* | *54%* |

**Table C**
Monthly analysis of winners 1969–84

| *Type of race* | | *Mar* | *Apr* | *May* | *Jun* | *Jul* | *Aug* | *Sep* | *Oct* | *Nov* | *Total* |
|---|---|---|---|---|---|---|---|---|---|---|---|
| Pattern Races | (Older horses) | – | 6 | 8 | 14 | 8 | 3 | 5 | 4 | 1 | 49 |
| Handicaps | (Older horses) | – | 11 | 12 | 8 | 12 | 8 | 1 | 1 | – | 53 |
| Other Races | (Older horses) | 2 | 4 | 12 | 2 | 8 | 7 | 9 | 3 | – | 47 |
| *Total* | *(Older horses)* | *2* | *21* | *32* | *24* | *28* | *18* | *15* | *8* | *1* | *149* |
| Pattern Races | (3-year-olds) | – | 14 | 14 | 12 | 8 | 8 | 6 | 5 | – | 67 |
| Handicaps | (3-year-olds) | – | 19 | 15 | 21 | 37 | 24 | 26 | 6 | 1 | 149 |
| Other Races | (3-year-olds) | 1 | 8 | 23 | 14 | 22 | 23 | 31 | 16 | – | 138 |
| Maidens | (3-year-olds) | 1 | 50 | 48 | 36 | 56 | 27 | 19 | 8 | – | 245 |
| *Total* | *(3-year-olds)* | *2* | *91* | *100* | *83* | *123* | *82* | *82* | *35* | *1* | *599* |
| Pattern Races | (2-year-olds) | – | – | – | 2 | 5 | 2 | 12 | 11 | 1 | 33 |
| Nurseries | (2-year-olds) | – | – | – | – | – | 7 | 9 | 2 | – | 18 |
| Other Races | (2-year-olds) | – | 9 | 29 | 44 | 97 | 90 | 76 | 56 | 9 | 410 |
| *Total* | *(2-year-olds)* | – | *9* | *29* | *46* | *102* | *99* | *97* | *69* | *10* | *461* |
| *Overall total* | | *4* | *121* | *161* | *153* | *253* | *199* | *194* | *112* | *12* | *1,209* |

| *Year* | *Mar* | *Apr* | *May* | *Jun* | *Jul* | *Aug* | *Sep* | *Oct* | *Nov* | *Total* |
|---|---|---|---|---|---|---|---|---|---|---|
| 1969 | – | – | 2 | 5 | 5 | 4 | 9 | 2 | – | 27 |
| 1970 | – | 2 | 6 | 5 | 14 | 3 | 4 | 1 | – | 35 |
| 1971 | – | 14 | 9 | 7 | 12 | 2 | 7 | 2 | – | 53 |
| 1972 | 3 | 6 | 2 | 3 | 16 | 8 | 8 | 5 | 2 | 53 |
| 1973 | 1 | 13 | 5 | 4 | 3 | 5 | 4 | 6 | – | 41 |
| 1974 | – | 6 | 10 | 4 | 17 | 7 | 4 | 2 | – | 50 |
| 1975 | – | 5 | 10 | 11 | 18 | 19 | 7 | 12 | – | 82 |
| 1976 | – | 5 | 7 | 5 | 16 | 11 | 6 | 2 | – | 52 |
| 1977 | – | 7 | 12 | 6 | 13 | 14 | 17 | 5 | – | 74 |
| 1978 | – | 5 | 15 | 15 | 28 | 18 | 15 | 13 | 1 | 110 |
| 1979 | – | 9 | 16 | 18 | 21 | 24 | 18 | 17 | 5 | 128 |
| 1980 | – | 5 | 20 | 13 | 14 | 17 | 11 | 3 | 2 | 85 |
| 1981 | – | 11 | 11 | 17 | 16 | 17 | 23 | 12 | 1 | 108 |
| 1982 | – | 16 | 14 | 13 | 22 | 13 | 22 | 11 | – | 111 |
| 1983 | – | 8 | 8 | 11 | 22 | 16 | 17 | 10 | – | 92 |
| 1984 | – | 9 | 14 | 16 | 16 | 21 | 22 | 9 | 1 | 108 |
| *Total* | *4* | *121* | *161* | *153* | *253* | *199* | *194* | *112* | *12* | *1,209* |

**Table D**

Most successful racecourses

*All races*

188 Newmarket
127 Yarmouth
69 Nottingham
65 Newbury
64 Ascot
(including 31 at Royal Ascot)
63 Goodwood
55 Leicester
45 York
39 Sandown
34 Warwick
34 Windsor
34 Wolverhampton
30 Haydock
29 Beverley
26 Catterick
24 Pontefract
22 Kempton
22 Redcar
21 Newcastle
17 Brighton
17 Lingfield
17 Thirsk
16 Chester
15 Ripon
15 Epsom
13 Ayr
12 Folkestone
7 Abroad
+9 Other Racecourses with 6 winners or less each.

*Pattern races*

36 Ascot
(including 25 at Royal Ascot)
31 Newmarket
16 Doncaster
14 Newbury
13 Goodwood
11 York
9 Sandown

5 Abroad
5 Epsom
4 Chester
2 Lingfield
2 Haydock
1 Kempton

**Table E**
Most successful jockeys

*All races*
369 L. Piggott
310 J. Mercer
138 G. Starkey
66 A. Bond
62 N. Day
34 Paul Eddery
32 F. Durr
20 G. Dettori
18 J. Higgins
15 M. Thomas
12 Pat Eddery
10 J. Cecil
9 S. Cauthen
8 P. Cook
8 G. Baxter
8 W. Carson
8 B. Raymond
7 A. Kimberley
7 G. Lewis
6 E. Hide
6 B. Taylor
4 E. Eldin
4 A. Murray
4 G. Sexton
3 J. Seagrave
3 S. Smith
3 W. Swinburne
+29 Other Jockeys with 2 winners each or less.

*Pattern races*
69 L. Piggott
52 J. Mercer
13 G. Dettori

7 G. Starkey
3 Pat Eddery
2 A. Bond
2 Paul Eddery
1 G. Baxter
1 D. Keith
1 S. Cauthen

**Table F**
Best horses trained 1969–84

| *First prize money* | | *Total prize money* | |
|---|---|---|---|
| Ardross | £278,127.00 | Ardross | £349,852.95 |
| Wollow | £200,789.75 | Wollow | £200,789.75 |
| Kris | £168,953.95 | Kris | £195,670.45 |
| Le Moss | £147,652.40 | Le Moss | £173,436.41 |
| Light Cavalry | £118,691.60 | Light Cavalry | £139,044.48 |
| Hello Gorgeous | £ 97,351.60 | Hello Gorgeous | £129,646.00 |
| Dunbeath | £ 91,081.80 | Gunner B | £111,424.35 |
| Diesis | £ 88,649.60 | Dunbeath | £ 92,257.80 |
| Gunner B | £ 84,307.60 | Adonijah | £ 96,903.75 |
| Chalon | £ 82,276.95 | Salieri | £ 94,934.80 |

| *Races won* | | *Pattern races won* | |
|---|---|---|---|
| Kris | 14 | Ardross | 11 |
| Fool's Mate | 13 | Kris | 8 |
| Ardross | 11 | Le Moss | 7 |
| Le Moss | 11 | Wollow | 7 |
| Arisaig | 10 | Gunner B | 4 |
| Francesco | 10 | Roussalka | 4 |
| Amboise | 9 | Salieri | 4 |
| Irvine | 9 | | |
| Wollow | 9 | | |

| *Percentage wins/races* | | *Percentage places/races* | |
|---|---|---|---|
| Kris | 88% | Kris | 100% |
| Wollow | 82% | Ardross | 93% |
| Ardross | 79% | Sea Music | 91% |
| Le Moss | 73% | Le Moss | 87% |
| Sea Music | 73% | Amboise | 84% |
| Chalon | 70% | Falkland | 83% |
| Crack of Light | 57% | Odeon | 83% |
| Barwin | 50% | Light Cavalry | 82% |
| Home on the Range | 50% | Wollow | 82% |
| Katie Cecil | 50% | Chalon | 80% |

**Table G**

Most successful owners 1969–84

| *First prize money* | | *Total prize money* | |
|---|---|---|---|
| C. St George | £698,761.35 | C. St George | £900,049.95 |
| C. d'Alessio | £657,819.19 | D. Wildenstein | £831,903.37 |
| D. Wildenstein | £615,251.05 | C. d'Alessio | £767,624.83 |
| Lord Howard de Walden | £472,425.77 | Lord Howard de Walden | £613,298.16 |
| H. J. Joel | £382,302.85 | H. J. Joel | £488,951.34 |
| M. D. Riordan | £196,469.45 | L. Freedman | £252,743.41 |
| L. Freedman | £169,991.90 | M. D. Riordan | £199,695.25 |
| Lord Tavistock | £107,530.50 | Shiekh Mohammed | £192,581.35 |
| Sheikh Mohammed | £105,669.20 | S. Niarchos | £120,813.75 |
| S. Niarchos | £ 92,303.45 | Lord Tavistock | £116,779.90 |

| *Races won* | | *Pattern race won* | |
|---|---|---|---|
| D. Wildenstein | 123 | C. d'Alessio | 26 |
| C. St George | 112 | C. St George | 24 |
| Lord Howard de Walden | 101 | Lord Howard de Walden | 16 |
| C. d'Alessio | 89 | D. Wildenstein | 15 |
| H. J. Joel | 84 | H. J. Joel | 9 |
| Sir R. Macdonald-Buchanan | 61 | M. D. Riordan | 6 |
| L. Freedman | 43 | Lord Tavistock | 5 |
| S. Niarchos | 24 | | |

| *Percentage wins/races* | | *Percentage places/races* | |
|---|---|---|---|
| M. D. Riordan | 45% | H. Barker | 80% |
| H. Demetriou | 44% | S. Niarchos | 76% |
| Mrs G. Lambton | 43% | Sheikh Mohammed | 74% |
| N. Barker | 41% | Lady Mairi Bury | 68% |
| S. Niarchos | 41% | Mrs G. Lambton | 68% |
| P. Burrell | 38% | M. D. Riordan | 68% |
| C. d'Alessio | 37% | C. d'Alessio | 67% |

**Table H**
Most successful sires of horses trained 1969–84

| *First prize money* | | *Total prize money* | |
|---|---|---|---|
| Sharpen Up | £315,528.85 | Run The Gauntlet | £373,939.85 |
| Run The Gauntlet | £296,668.20 | Sharpen Up | £372,568.39 |
| Habitat | £280,513.20 | Habitat | £317,915.43 |
| Mill Reef | £221,126.00 | Mill Reef | £279,179.79 |
| Wolver Hollow | £215,149.05 | Wolver Hollow | £218,374.95 |
| Brigadier Gerard | £173,735.20 | Brigadier Gerard | £200,317.28 |
| Le Levanstell | £147,859.40 | Le Levanstell | £173,963.01 |
| Lyphard | £111,329.25 | Lyphard | £171,257.09 |
| Relko | £103,018.80 | Mr Prospector | £135,048.10 |
| Mr Prospector | £101,107.30 | Relko | £132,489.70 |

| *Races won* | | *Pattern races won* | |
|---|---|---|---|
| Busted | 41 | Sharpen Up | 14 |
| Habitat | 40 | Habitat | 11 |
| Mill Reef | 26 | Run The Gauntlet | 11 |
| Sharpen Up | 25 | Le Levanstell | 7 |
| Lyphard | 22 | Mill Reef | 7 |
| Connaught | 19 | Wolver Hollow | 7 |
| Reform | 19 | Brigadier Gerard | 6 |
| Run The Gauntlet | 19 | | |
| Welsh Pageant | 19 | | |

| *Percentage wins/races* | | *Percentage places/races* | |
|---|---|---|---|
| Sharpen Up | 64% | Sharpen Up | 87% |
| Caro | 41% | Alcide | 71% |
| Lorenzaccio | 40% | Relko | 70% |
| Habitat | 38% | Connaught | 69% |
| Luthier | 38% | Run The Gauntlet | 68% |
| Run The Gauntlet | 38% | Northern Dancer | 67% |
| Shirley Heights | 38% | Vaguely Noble | 67% |

**Table I**
Betting analysis 1969–84 (to a £10 level stake)

| *Year* | *Older Horses* | *3 Year Olds* | *2 Year Olds* | *Total* |
|---|---|---|---|---|
| 1969 | −£115.00 | −£ 90.40 | +£ 265.40 | +£ 60.00 |
| 1970 | +£166.20 | +£ 35.50 | −£ 301.30 | −£ 99.60 |
| 1971 | −£106.70 | −£258.00 | −£ 303.70 | −£668.40 |
| 1972 | −£165.60 | −£468.60 | +£ 302.50 | −£331.70 |
| 1973 | −£ 72.10 | −£221.40 | +£ 341.20 | +£ 47.70 |
| 1974 | −£142.10 | +£ 55.30 | +£ 2.80 | −£ 84.00 |
| 1975 | −£ 79.20 | +£305.90 | +£ 107.30 | +£334.00 |
| 1976 | +£ 17.10 | −£295.00 | −£ 181.60 | −£459.50 |
| 1977 | −£125.20 | +£317.80 | −£ 342.60 | −£150.00 |
| 1978 | +£ 50.70 | +£ 96.00 | +£ 197.50 | +£344.20 |
| 1979 | +£125.00 | +£356.90 | +£ 221.60 | +£703.50 |
| 1980 | −£ 87.70 | −£442.20 | +£ 240.30 | −£289.60 |
| 1981 | +£208.90 | +£277.40 | +£ 485.90 | +£972.20 |
| 1982 | −£208.30 | −£ 93.30 | +£ 202.60 | −£ 99.00 |
| 1983 | +£107.30 | −£ 86.30 | −£ 87.30 | −£ 66.30 |
| 1984 | +£ 24.00 | −£143.10 | −£ 6.80 | −£125.90 |
| *Totals* | −£402.70 | −£653.50 | +£1,143.80 | +£ 87.60 |

**Table J**
Average weight carried by handicap winners 1969–84

| *Year* | *Handicap winners* | *Average weight carried* |
|---|---|---|
| 1969 | 10 | 8st 2lbs |
| 1970 | 10 | 8st 7lbs |
| 1971 | 12 | 8st 9lbs |
| 1972 | 10 | 8st 8lbs |
| 1973 | 11 | 8st 10lbs |
| 1974 | 11 | 8st 9lbs |
| 1975 | 20 | 8st 13lbs |
| 1976 | 14 | 9st 3lbs |
| 1977 | 25 | 8st 11lbs |
| 1978 | 15 | 8st 12lbs |
| 1979 | 22 | 9st 1lb |
| 1980 | 13 | 9st 3lbs |
| 1981 | 19 | 9st 2lbs |
| 1982 | 10 | 9st 3lbs |
| 1983 | 6 | 9st 2lbs |
| 1984 | 12 | 9st 1lbs |
| *Total* | *220* | *8st 12lbs* |

**Table K**
Winners on seasonal debut 1969–84

| *Year* | *Age group* | *Winners* | *Runners* | *Percentage* |
|---|---|---|---|---|
| 1969 | Older Horses | – | 9 | – |
| | 3 year olds | – | 15 | – |
| | 2 year olds | 1 | 14 | 7% |
| | *Total* | *1* | *38* | *3%* |
| 1970 | Older Horses | 1 | 6 | 17% |
| | 3 year olds | 1 | 23 | 4% |
| | 2 year olds | 2 | 22 | 9% |
| | *Total* | *4* | *51* | *8%* |
| 1971 | Older Horses | – | 5 | – |
| | 3 year olds | 7 | 22 | 32% |
| | 2 year olds | 5 | 34 | 15% |
| | *Total* | *12* | *61* | *20%* |
| 1972 | Older Horses | 4 | 6 | 66% |
| | 3 year olds | 4 | 33 | 12% |
| | 2 year olds | 4 | 27 | 15% |
| | *Total* | *12* | *66* | *18%* |
| 1973 | Older Horses | 1 | 4 | 25% |
| | 3 year olds | 7 | 32 | 22% |
| | 2 year olds | 2 | 21 | 10% |
| | *Total* | *10* | *57* | *18%* |
| 1974 | Older Horses | 1 | 7 | 14% |
| | 3 year olds | 4 | 26 | 15% |
| | 2 year olds | 6 | 31 | 19% |
| | *Total* | *11* | *64* | *17%* |
| 1975 | Older Horses | 1 | 9 | – |
| | 3 year olds | 4 | 32 | 13% |
| | 2 year olds | 8 | 33 | 24% |
| | *Total* | *13* | *74* | *17%* |
| 1976 | Older Horses | 1 | 6 | 17% |
| | 3 year olds | 4 | 29 | 14% |
| | 2 year olds | 5 | 27 | 19% |
| | *Total* | *10* | *62* | *16%* |

| | | | | |
|---|---|---|---|---|
| 1977 | Older Horses | 1 | 9 | 11% |
| | 3 year olds | 10 | 40 | 15% |
| | 2 year olds | 3 | 32 | 9% |
| | *Total* | *14* | *81* | *17%* |
| 1978 | Older Horses | 6 | 15 | 40% |
| | 3 year olds | 10 | 38 | 26% |
| | 2 year olds | 8 | 36 | 22% |
| | *Total* | *24* | *89* | *27%* |
| 1979 | Older Horses | 3 | 4 | 75% |
| | 3 year olds | 15 | 36 | 40% |
| | 2 year olds | 16 | 34 | 47% |
| | *Total* | *34* | *74* | *46%* |
| 1980 | Older Horses | 2 | 11 | 18% |
| | 3 year olds | 11 | 48 | 23% |
| | 2 year olds | 9 | 35 | 26% |
| | *Total* | *22* | *94* | *23%* |
| 1981 | Older Horses | 3 | 8 | 37% |
| | 3 year olds | 11 | 35 | 31% |
| | 2 year olds | 14 | 53 | 26% |
| | *Total* | *28* | *96* | *29%* |
| 1982 | Older Horses | 2 | 7 | 29% |
| | 3 year olds | 13 | 42 | 31% |
| | 2 year olds | 15 | 47 | 32% |
| | *Total* | *30* | *96* | *31%* |
| 1983 | Older Horses | 2 | 5 | 40% |
| | 3 year olds | 9 | 43 | 21% |
| | 2 year olds | 19 | 56 | 34% |
| | *Total* | *30* | *104* | *29%* |
| 1984 | Older Horses | 2 | 5 | 40% |
| | 3 year olds | 13 | 53 | 25% |
| | 2 year olds | 19 | 50 | 38% |
| | *Total* | *34* | *108* | *31%* |
| *Total* | Older Horses | 30 | 116 | 26% |
| | 3 year olds | 123 | 547 | 22% |
| | 2 year olds | 136 | 552 | 25% |
| | *Overall total* | *289* | *1,215* | *24%* |

**Table L**
Monthly record of debut performance 1969–84

| *Month* | *Older Horses* | *3 Year Olds* | *2 Year Olds* | *Total* |
|---|---|---|---|---|
| Mar+Apr | 22% Winners | 22% Winners | 41% Winners | 23% Winners |
| May | 21% Winners | 19% Winners | 34% Winners | 24% Winners |
| June | 40% Winners | 23% Winners | 27% Winners | 27% Winners |
| July | 0% Winners | 32% Winners | 24% Winners | 26% Winners |
| August | 40% Winners | 29% Winners | 25% Winners | 26% Winners |
| September | 100% Winners | 16% Winners | 21% Winners | 22% Winners |
| Oct+Nov | 100% Winners | 100% Winners | 17% Winners | 19% Winners |
| *Total* | *26% Winners* | *22% Winners* | *25% Winners* | *24% Winners* |

Betting on debut performances 1969–84 (at S.P. to a £10 level stake)

| *Year* | *Older Horses* | *3 Year Olds* | *2 Year Olds* | *Total* |
|---|---|---|---|---|
| 1969 | −£ 90.00 | −£150.00 | −£ 30.00 | −£270.00 |
| 1970 | +£150.00 | −£165.00 | −£ 70.00 | −£ 85.00 |
| 1971 | −£ 50.00 | +£ 35.10 | −£128.70 | −£143.60 |
| 1972 | +£ 55.00 | −£ 83.70 | +£172.50 | +£143.80 |
| 1973 | −£ 16.30 | −£147.70 | +£195.00 | +£ 31.00 |
| 1974 | −£ 42.50 | +£253.80 | +£249.40 | +£460.70 |
| 1975 | −£ 35.00 | −£122.00 | −£ 72.70 | −£229.70 |
| 1976 | −£ 60.00 | −£145.90 | −£ 71.80 | −£277.70 |
| 1977 | −£ 52.50 | +£ 23.50 | −£199.00 | +£228.00 |
| 1978 | +£ 93.30 | +£262.50 | −£ 25.20 | +£330.60 |
| 1979 | +£ 74.10 | +£200.50 | +£ 99.20 | +£373.80 |
| 1980 | −£ 56.40 | −£ 6.40 | −£ 55.40 | −£118.20 |
| 1981 | +£ 70.00 | +£ 68.90 | +£213.40 | +£351.30 |
| 1982 | −£ 30.00 | +£ 83.70 | +£ 49.20 | +£102.90 |
| 1983 | +£ 73.30 | −£ 57.80 | −£ 9.40 | +£ 6.10 |
| 1984 | +£ 65.00 | −£ 52.90 | +£138.60 | +£150.70 |
| *Total* | +£148.00 | −£ 3.40 | +£454.10 | +£598.70 |

# Index

NOTE: *references to myself, to my stepfather, Captain Sir Cecil Boyd-Rochfort, to my father-in-law, Sir Noel Murless, and to my wife, Julie, are not indexed because of their frequency.*